THE CONCEPT OF EXPRESSION

THE CONCEPT OF Expression

A STUDY IN
PHILOSOPHICAL
PSYCHOLOGY
AND AESTHETICS

ALAN TORMEY

PRINCETON UNIVERSITY PRESS
1971

This book has been composed in Linotype Granjon

Printed in the United States of America
by Princeton University Press
Princeton, New Jersey

FOR JUDITH

FOREWORD

THE CONCEPT OF expression, to the philosophical clarification of which Professor Tormey's lucid essay is so successfully addressed, is notoriously vague at its boundaries and various in its senses. But one of its meanings is perhaps sufficiently stable that I may use it to support a few collateral reflections on expression. Since these converge with Tormey's analysis, they may serve to preface his contribution. No other *kind* of preface, with a work so clearly written and tautly argued, would be fitting.

In music, expression is that which accounts for the possibility of artistically distinct performances of the identical work: it is what the *performer* contributes in his capacity as a collaborative medium through which the notated score is transmuted into the shape of sound. If the score defines the work, then the performance is work plus expression or, in mock algebraic equivalence, expression is what remains when we subtract the work from a given performance. And since the work is a constant, artistic variations from performance to performance are due to variations in expression. The degree of permissible expressive variation has fluctuated from epoch to epoch of musical history, but composers who may be concerned with maximal uniformity in the class of performances of their works have sought to achieve this by an increasingly explicit set of directives governing cadence, phrasing, and dynamics—matters more casually left to the decision of the performer in a more permissive atmosphere. At times, indeed, so much was left to the performer that identification of two performances as *of* the same work was an almost metaphysical achievement.

The artistic autonomy of the performer varies as a function of the explicitness of the expressive directions, but for reasons too complex to enter upon here, it cannot be eliminated or reduced to zero. Radical options are, of course, available to the composer obsessed with expressive conformity: he may, for example, work directly in sound, like an acoustical sculptor. Artistically distinct performances of the same work are here ruled out through identifying the work with the performance in such a way that distinct performances are distinct works. But short of this radical displacement of the middleman, which is achieved by crossing a logical boundary into another genre of creation, composers must acquiesce in something being an expression of a work only if something else, artistically distinct from it, also may be counted an expression of that same work. The work then gives an identity to an open species of expressions, subject to mutations and evolution. The score stands to the species thus generated in something like the logical relation in which Platonic Ideas were supposed to stand to their instances and embodiments in the mutable world.

Suppose we indulge ourselves by viewing the performer as expressing a musical idea in the shape of sound. Then we might extend this conception to the other arts by taking certain remarkable liberties. A set of poems may take their identity through being, perhaps, artistically distinct expressions of the same thought or idea; a set of paintings is identified by an idea of which they are artistically distinct expressions. In poetry and in painting alike, *expression* then may be reckoned that which the artist contributes in transmuting ideas into the forms of rhythms and paint, mediator and maker at once.

At times, artists have been under the domination of a platonistic ideology of art and have aimed at an absolute self-effacement. An audience is supposed to be put in direct confrontation with *what* is expressed, without being distracted by the expression of it. Thus the pianist aims at a perfect transparency in favor of the music; the actress Berma kept disappearing in favor of Phèdre, the character she portrayed, much to the consternation of the Narrator of Proust's book, who came to see, not to see *through*, the acting. So words are not to distract us from the idea they express, and paint is to vanish in the illusion of, say, the Angel of the Annunciation. Audiences initially hostile to Cézanne saw him as a distorting lens, warping the surfaces of apples and mountains, standing opaquely (and hence ineptly) between audience and what he was supposed to reveal. And when the early apologists, like Roger Fry, explained that Cézanne and his peers were more concerned with expression itself than the *idea* (or seeming idea) to which transparent artists had by contrast submerged themselves, this was like a Copernican revolution, reorienting the entire universe of art! Appreciation revolved now around expression, and even cameras were introduced into scenes they formerly were external recorders of, caressing the star, exploring the room, seeking out and recoiling, filling the spaces they were designed to vacate.

A Copernican revolution in artistic perception naturally entailed a revolution in historical perception as well, for it became plain that art never had been transparent. Once one began to seek them out in the space between audience and idea, artists emerged from their works like resurrected bodies in that Day of Judgment depicted in the central tympanum of Notre Dame. The most transparent artists, men whose technical achievement had been, like Parahesios, to render technique indiscernible, became expressively opaque, to the detriment of the illusions they had sought and the ideas to which they had sacrificed themselves. Transfigurations and Descents receded in favor of their expressions, and the attempt must inevitably have been made to distill out an art which was *pure* expression. Abstract Expressionism, indeed, was heralded as the final purification and redemption of art.

In fact (and in logic), to be an expression is to be an expression *of* something, and ideas are in consequence inseparable from art. The idea of Abstract Expressionist painting was the idea of expression itself, so that art (or painting at least) became its own subject, which is what is distinctive of contemporary art. Abstract Expressionism was defined not only by the self-consciousness of its idea, but by an impoverished, narrow conception of what expression consists in—as though the idea of expression could only be expressed with thick paint, spills, drips, amplified brush-strokes, and the like. The extreme restrictiveness of this vocabulary (and the puritanical ideology which enforced it) was painfully exposed when it was displaced by the Post-Painterly art of the sixties, which repudiated Expressionist expression by conspicuously *not* employing it. The narrowness of that vocabulary of expression became part of the idea of Post-Painterly art, which was reflected in its use of mechanical, flat, hard-edged forms. This idea became explicit in an arch series of paintings *of* drips and *of* brush-strokes (which were painted without either drips or brush-strokes) by the Pop artist Roy Lichtenstein.

Post-Painterly art did not eliminate expression by breaking out of this externally constricted range of modes of expression, though it is natural that artists might have thought they had done this, and that they had created a counter-revolution by eliminating expression and making art a matter of pure idea. But the ideationalist artist (who is perhaps distinguished from a philosopher of art by the mere fact that he *exhibits* his ideas) has crossed much the same sort of boundary the acoustical sculptor did, into a distinct artistic space. For to resort to the expedient of only talking about works, rather than creating them (which is exactly the strategy of what today is called Conceptual Art), is to acknowledge the logical inseparability of expression from art. Art is a function of expression and idea, and the recent history of the subject is a comedy in which artists have sought to reduce, in a spirit of purity, one or the other argument of this function to zero.

Given that it is ineradicable, then, what is the philosophical status of expression?

In the philosophical psychologies of the seventeenth century, emotions were considered as ideas—*confused* ideas, according to Spinoza, but ideas even so. Hence the expression of an emotion would be the expression of a (confused) idea. Professor Tormey reactivates this sort of view by advancing a thesis that the expression of a feeling (or of a belief, or whatever) is the expression of an *intentional state*. Intentional states of persons can be reckoned ideas, in the elastic, seventeenth-century conception of them, and in this respect there may be a partial analogy between a person and a work of art. For works of art are expressions of ideas, or at least we may regard the logical relation of expression to idea as parallel in the case of persons and of works of art.

The theory that art *is* expression has always insisted upon something more striking than this (imperfect) structural analogy. It has insisted that the expression, which is the artist's contribution to the work of art, is *also* the expression of an internal (romantically visceral) state of himself, so that works of art are to be classed with sobs and sighs and like expressions of innerness, unless they just *are* sobs and sighs changed into something rich and strange. We are asked to believe that, in expressing an idea, the artist is expressing himself. In suggesting only a logical analogy between expressions and ideas in persons and in works of art, Tormey begins the destruction of that hopeless theory that works of art are the exudates of souls.

His book redeems, indeed, a number of crucial philosophical structures from the washlands of errors, puns, and sentimentalities which have governed and distorted our reflections upon expression and art. He makes these structures available now for an adequate philosophy of art and

mind. As suits a book on expression, it *exhibits* that lucidity of phrase and cadence to which expressions of philosophical ideas ought to aspire when philosophical prose
aspires to the status of art.

Arthur C. Danto

New York City

PREFACE

FEW TERMS IN the language have found more diversified use than 'expression'; and the occurrence of a single term in divergent roles is fair warning to the philosopher that clarity has been sacrificed to facility. No single work, of course, can hope to account for all the vagaries of 'expression,' but the present study is centered upon what is perhaps its most paradigmatic role: that of marking a relation between human behavior and certain characteristic states of a person. The nature of this relation is the heart of our story. No attempt has been made to trace the historical development of the concept or to track it through all its permutations in ordinary or philosophical usage. The aim has been rather to construct an analysis from the examination of typical forms of human expression and from the logical implications of our description of such expressions; and although no theoretical position is presupposed at the outset, something emerges in the process which I think may fairly be thought of as a theory of expression. The theory appears in outline in Chapters I and II, and is further extended to language in Chapter III and to art in Chapters IV and V.

I would like to thank O. K. Bouwsma, Peter Kivy, Richard F. Kuhns, Jr., and James J. Walsh, all of whom offered perceptive and illuminating comments on various drafts of this study. Sanford Thatcher of Princeton University Press has been an invaluable source of both philosophical and editorial advice in preparing the manuscript; and there are special and inexpressible debts of gratitude to Arthur

Danto whose encouragement tempered with rigorous critical reflections inspired the entire project, and to Judith
Tormey who has enriched both my philosophical thought
and my life more than I could hope to acknowledge, and
whose contributions to this work are inextricably woven
with my own.

Alan Tormey

New York, April 1970

CONTENTS

FOREWORD   vii
    BY ARTHUR DANTO

PREFACE   xv

   I.   Behavior and Expression   5

  II.   Inference and Expression   39

III.   Language and Expression   63

IV.   Art and Expression: A Critique   97

  V.   Art and Expression: A Proposal   127

APPENDIX   143

BIBLIOGRAPHY   153

INDEX   161

There are certain terms in scientific discussion which seem to make any advance impossible. They stupefy and bewilder, yet in a way satisfy, the inquiring mind, and though the despair of those who like to know what they have said, are the delight of all whose main concern with words is the avoidance of trouble. 'Expression' is such an one.

The Meaning of Meaning
Ogden and Richards

CHAPTER I BEHAVIOR AND
EXPRESSION

I | WE EXPRESS, both in our speech and our non-linguistic behavior, a prodigious variety of things, from beliefs and attitudes to moods, intentions, and emotions, from hope, hostility, and anger to pity, doubt, and elation. It is clear, however, that neither behavior nor language is expressive of everything that could be said to be a state of a person. We do not, for example, express our blood count, our temperature, our weight, or our age. Our first task then will be to distinguish those states of a person that are expressed, or expressible in language and behavior from those that are not, and to isolate if possible some condition or criterion for marking that distinction.

It is tempting to think that a criterion may already be available; and a glance at the random list above might suggest that whatever—and only whatever—shall count as a "psychological" or "mental" state of a person may be expressed in his behavior. But it may be plausibly objected that sensations and perceptions are more properly regarded as psychological or mental than as merely physical states of a person, and that it is not clear that we *express*, in any way, either our sensations or our perceptions. If this is the case then, the rough-hewn distinction between the mental and the physical will fail to provide an adequate criterion for marking the difference between expressible and nonexpressible states of a person. But this also suggests that a study of the differences between sensation (or perception) and such expressible states of a person as his attitudes and emotions may reveal the criterion we are seeking.

5

It does in fact appear that, whatever purpose we may have in speaking of the expression of other states of a person, we have no use for the concept of an expression of sensation. If our language is a reflection of our limitations then, we do not, and perhaps cannot, express our sensations.[1] (I shall assume that we can agree for the present to call such things as itches, throbs, warmth, pressure, bitter tastes, and acrid smells sensations. As I shall indicate later, an argument could be constructed similar to the one which follows, substituting 'perception' for 'sensation'; and it should be clear subsequently why the drawing of precise boundaries between sensation and perception is not critical for my argument.)

Let us explore then the possibility of locating some condition common to the occurrences of expression that will explain the exclusion of sensation from the list of states which are normally expressed in our behavior.

It will be expedient to call attention first to the absence of any clear or paradigmatic use for a linguistic reference to an expression of sensation. It would be something more than linguistic oddity to speak, for instance, of an expression of the sensation of heat. It is difficult in fact to imagine how such a sensation *could* be expressed. Should someone experiencing a sensation of heat cry out, open the window, or complain about the weather, these would be perfectly appropriate expressions of discomfort, but I do not think we would be constrained to say he was also

[1] The expression of pain appears to be a formidable exception; but it is a special case, and I shall reserve discussion of it for later (cf. Section 3, below).

6

expressing his sensation. It might be argued that sensations, like beliefs and emotions, can be expressed linguistically, and that the correct expression would be an utterance: 'I am hot,' or 'I have a sensation of heat.' But this fails to distinguish between reporting (or describing) and expressing a condition. If someone were to exclaim 'I have a peculiar throbbing in my leg,' he might be describing his sensation, expressing surprise, concern, or discomfort, asking for help, or pleading for sympathy; but we would not say he was also expressing his throbbing sensation.

This peculiarity at least should be noted: there do not appear to be any natural or appropriate behavioral expressions of sensation as there are of beliefs, attitudes, and emotions. There are of course *responses* to sensations that are wholly natural and appropriate, and there are causal consequences; but it would be merely perverse to call scratching the expression of an itch, or laughter the expression of a tickle. This should not prevent us from realizing that there are expressions which are associated in intimate ways with particular sensations. The odor of perfume may evoke an expression of desire, or the taste of the wine an expression of nostalgia. But these are not expressions of the *sensations*. They are expressions of attitudes, beliefs, feelings, or emotions which are occasioned *by* the sensations. Laughter occasioned by the hearing of a joke is an expression of amusement. But laughter occasioned by a tickle is neither the expression of amusement nor the expression of the tickle; it is not an expression at all.

7

It would be convenient if this were merely a question of causal relations such that we could say, for instance, that if Y is a cause of X (in some specified sense of 'cause'), then X cannot be an expression of Y. But we would need to show that the expressions of beliefs, attitudes, etc. are *never* caused by those beliefs and attitudes, and it is difficult to see how this could be done.

The introduction of causal relations at this point will contribute little toward the discovery of a relevant difference between sensations, and beliefs, attitudes, and feelings; and we are still faced with the problem of explaining the omission of sensations from the catalogue of mental or psychological states that are commonly expressed.

It might be thought that the salient difference between sensations and the expressible states of a person consists in the degree to which he "contributes" to them. Sensations happen to us (so the argument might go). We are only the passive neurological receiving mechanism for the stimuli that register particular atomic impressions, whereas we are able, frequently, to assume a more active role in forming or structuring our beliefs, our attitudes and even our emotions. We have less to say about the one than the others. But this proves too little, and the distinction itself rests on a questionable psychological theory. It is doubtful whether sensations are correctly described as impressions passively received by a neutral organism.[2] And it is not

[2] See e.g., D. O. Hebb: "Electrophysiology of the central nervous system indicates in brief that the brain is continuously active, in all its parts, and an afferent excitation must be superimposed on an already existent excitation. It is therefore impossible that the consequence of a sensory event should be uninfluenced by the

evident that we play an "active" role in the structuring of every individual belief, attitude, or emotion. An attitude developed by strict behavioral conditioning would hardly merit this description. Nor is it clear how this difference, even if it were supportable, could explain why beliefs are expressed and sensations are not.

Other forms of asymmetry may seem more promising. It might be suggested that the difference can be accounted for by pointing out that beliefs, attitudes, and emotions are present dispositionally as well as being immediate constituents of consciousness, while sensations must exist as the immediate constituents of consciousness, or not at all. There are no variant forms for the existence of sensations; they are simply the primitive and atomic material of consciousness. As a corollary of this, beliefs and attitudes are sustained over long periods of time, compared with the passing and momentary existence of sensations.

Here again, however, the distinction itself is suspect. It is not obvious that every emotion or belief is present dispositionally. There are ephemeral feelings and fugitive beliefs, and emotions that flourish only once and never recur. And there are enduring sensations. A passing fancy is no less real than an interminable flutter. And here too it is difficult to see how we should be helped if we could employ this contrast in good faith. Duration and disposition are neither the guarantee nor the death of expression. A pass-

---

pre-existent activity . . . so there really is a rational basis for postulating a central neural factor that modifies the action of a stimulus" (*The Organization of Behavior: A Neuropsychological Theory* [New York: Wiley, 1949], p. 7).

ing belief or a sudden joy may find expression, but even a lasting or recurrent sensation cannot.

A more promising difference arises from the observation that beliefs, attitudes, and emotions have objects, while sensations do not. We can describe this difference by noting that sensations, unlike beliefs, attitudes and emotions have no *intentional objects*. I think we may use this terminology to explore the present issue without engaging in extended dispute over the much debated ontological status of intentional objects;[3] and in order to avoid this, as well as similar difficulties generated by previous analyses of intentionality, I propose to define an intentional object as whatever is designated by the *prepositional*

---

[3] An idea of the extent of this problem can be gained from E. Husserl, *Logische Untersuchungen*, 2 vols. (Halle: Max Niemeyer, 1900-1901) and Franz Brentano, *Wahrheit und Evidenz* (translated as *The True and the Evident* by Chisholm, Politzer, and Fischer [London: Routledge & Kegan Paul, 1966]). Brentano is largely responsible for reviving the scholastic notion of an intentional object and introducing it into modern philosophical discourse. In a letter to Anton Marty on the "so called 'immanent or intentional objects,'" Brentano says that ". . . by an *object* of thought I meant what it is that the thought is about whether or not there is anything outside the mind corresponding to the thought" (*The True and the Evident*, p. 77). The extension of 'thought' in Brentano's work appears to include wishes, desires, doubts, and dislikes. See R. Chisholm, *Perceiving* (Ithaca: Cornell, 1957), Ch. 11, for an explication of Brentano's concept of intentional inexistence, and the excerpts from Brentano and Meinong in *Realism and the Background of Phenomenology*, ed. R. Chisholm (New York: The Free Press, 1960). There are attempts to exorcise the problem in W.V.O. Quine's *Word and Object* (New York: Technology Press of MIT and Wiley, 1960) and Israel Scheffler's *The Anatomy of Inquiry* (New York: Knopf, 1963).

object of a particular mental act, state, or attitude. (More precisely, an intentional object is whatever is designated by a prepositional object occurring in a sentence used to ascribe some such state to a person. The ellipsis, once this is understood, should cause no confusion.)

If I am fascinated *by* centaurs, apprehensive *over* money, angry *with* the cook, or afraid *of* the dark, then centaurs, money, the cook, and the dark are the intentional objects of these states. Two points should be noted about the status of an intentional object as the concept will be employed here. First, there may or may not be anything in the world to which an intentional object corresponds. If I am greatly interested in the Hippogriff, it does not follow that there is or that there is not some creature that answers to the description of the Hippogriff, though it remains true to say that the Hippogriff is the (intentional) object of my interest. More generally, the truth of an intentional ascription such as '*A* is interested in witches' does not entail the truth of another statement asserting the existence of witches, as the truth of the nonintentional statement '*A* is walking in the garden' requires that there *be* a garden for *A* to walk in.[4] And, secondly, the description of an intentional object is a function of what the person himself *takes* to be the attributes of whatever he admires, wishes, fears, or is angry with. If I am angered by your insolence and deceit, it does not follow that you have in fact been insolent and deceitful, but only that I believe

---

[4] See Chisholm, *Perceiving*, Ch. 11, for a further defense of this distinction.

that you have and that I have taken or mistaken your actions in that light.

Now it may appear that to specify intentionality by reference to prepositional objects is unduly restrictive since it is not the case that all ascriptions of psychological states or mental processes have the sort of prepositional form that I have used to illustrate the definition. Both '*A* greatly admires surgeons' and '*B* distrusts musicians' lack the requisite prepositional syntax. This is not a serious objection however, since in such cases an equivalent ascription could be employed which *would* exemplify the required prepositional structure. '*A* has great admiration for surgeons' and '*B* is distrustful of musicians' will replace the nonprepositional formulations without alteration of meaning. And wherever it is possible to restructure such ascriptions to conform to this syntax, the prepositional object, I shall say, designates the intentional object of the mental state or process denoted in the ascription.

The most apparent threat to the plausibility of a prepositional analysis of intentionality is posed by statements of the form '*A* believes that *p*,' and it will be pertinent therefore to illustrate how such statements may be paraphrased or translated to conform to a prepositional structure. I shall offer an example of a typical belief attribution and three alternative translations into prepositional form. I am not for the moment concerned with deciding which of the translations is preferable on philosophical grounds, but only with the possibility of exhibiting the intentionality of such statements by effecting a translation that will permit the location of a prepositional object.

S Karl believes that ghosts exist.

   T_1 Karl believes in the existence of ghosts.

   T_2 Karl believes in the truth of the sentence 'Ghosts exist.'

   T_3 Karl assents (or is disposed to assent) to the proposition that ghosts exist.

T_1, T_2, and T_3, although of varying degrees of unnaturalness, preserve the normal truth conditions for *S* and at the same time clearly indicate the intentionality of the ascription. If such belief ascriptions—and 'that . . .' constructions in general—can be given similar prepositional paraphrasis, then a major objection to the scope of the definition will be removed. I shall proceed on the assumption that similar translations *can* be provided for analogous constructions, and that the definition will be vindicated to the extent that this proves to be possible.

And at this point we may introduce an ancillary definition. To say of a person that *he* is in an *intentional state* is to say that some sentence radical of this logical type may be truly predicated of him. Thus, if 'is hoping for salvation' is true of Gemma, then Gemma is in a particular intentional state.

These definitions are intended to ensure a measure of epistemological neutrality among competing analyses of mental or psychological states; and it is just such difficulties that I want to obviate at the outset since they are not immediately relevant to the analysis of expression.

At the very least then, there appears to be some point in speaking of beliefs, attitudes, and emotions as having

13

intentional objects and no point whatever in speaking of the objects of sensations. Admiration for Bartok, approval of socialism, affection for owls, and interest in archaeology are intentional states that are, truly or falsely, predicated of persons. But sensations are not about, for, or toward anything, and consequently, they are not intentional.[5]

This may escape attention since sensations are *of* something and 'of' is a preposition. We speak of a sensation of dizziness just as we would speak of a feeling of anger or an attitude of hostility. But the 'of' is systematically ambiguous. Anger is not the object of my feeling, nor is hostility the object of my attitude, and dizziness is not the object of my sensation.

In each case we could omit the preposition and rephrase the expression. We could have spoken with equal propriety of a dizzy sensation, an angry feeling, and a hostile attitude. But while hostile attitudes and angry feelings are directed toward 'objects' from which they are logically distinguishable, a sensation cannot be directed at anything. In the case of dizziness the sensation is not logically separable from the dizziness; it is a sensation-of-dizziness. A sensation has its logical terminus in the mere awareness of its presence, in simply being had. Compare, e.g. (1) 'sensation of heat' with (2) 'fear of darkness.' The 'of' is transitive in (2), but not in (1). Heat is not the object of the sensation as darkness is the object of the fear.[6]

[5] It is sometimes thought that not all emotions and feeling states are intentional; that anxiety, for example, is an "objectless fear." I shall return to this question in Section 5.

[6] For convenience, I shall use the terms 'transitive' and 'intransitive' to mark this distinction. Transitive and intransitive occur-

We are now in a position to explain why sensations are nonintentional in spite of the occurrence of the preposition in such expressions as 'sensation of cold' or 'sensation of dizziness.' 'Sensation' functions, logically, at the same level as 'emotion' or 'attitude' and not at the level of, say, 'fear' or 'hostility.' Thus, 'sensation of cold,' 'emotion (or feeling) of fear,' and 'attitude of hostility' are logically similar constructions. The 'of' is intransitive in all three, and there are no intentional objects in these expressions. However, it would be possible to go on, in the latter two instances, to ask 'fear *of* what?' and 'hostility *toward* what?' Here the prepositions are transitive, and an answer to these questions will denote the intentional objects of the fear and the hostility. In contrast, we cannot go on to ask in the first case 'cold of what?' or 'dizziness of what?'

The locution 'sensation of . . .' is used to specify the *kind* of sensation that is meant, just as to talk of a feeling of anger is to say what sort of feeling it is, and not to name an object of the feeling. It is the *particular* feeling or attitude that has an object, and it is just here, with respect to particular sensations, that we cannot pursue the parallel question. Here there is no possibility for the occurrence of a transitive preposition and thus no possibility that sensations have intentional objects.

It is true that we do not express our perceptions either, and an argument could be given, parallel to the one above,

---

rences of 'of' correspond closely to the grammatical distinction between subjective and objective genitive case functions. See e.g. Barbara M. H. Strang, *Modern English Structure* (London: Edward Arnold, 1962), Ch. vi.

substituting 'perception' for 'sensation.' This is not to say that sensation and perception differ in no important way; indeed, the differences have been a constant source of anxiety in Anglo-American philosophy. My point is rather that they differ insufficiently to affect the present argument. There is of course a difference between feeling hot and feeling the radiator, or seeing spots and seeing the piano. Perceiving normally implies an object perceived and the perception verbs—'see,' 'hear,' 'feel,' and so on—require *direct* objects. But this does not certify acts of perception as intentional in the sense appropriate to beliefs, attitudes, or feelings. The objects of my perceivings are not prepositional, and thus not intentional. My perceptions are not about, for, over, from, in, or toward anything in the sense in which I have beliefs about centaurs, hostility toward hypocrites, admiration for Bartok, and misgivings over politics. Perceptions cannot be granted or withheld like beliefs, nor fulfilled or frustrated like desires. They cannot be justified, renounced, adopted, cultivated, or misguided; and, like sensations, they cannot be expressed.

Finally, we can distinguish between the causes and the objects of such states as hatred, fear, and faith.[7] The child believes *in* Santa Claus *because* her father has assured her he exists. Sensations have causes, but no objects. If I choose to call the tickling in my arm 'sensing a feather,' I am assigning a cause to the sensation, not mentioning an

---

[7] Cf. Wittgenstein's remark: "We should distinguish between the object of fear and the cause of fear. . . . Thus a face which inspires fear or delight (the object of fear or delight), is not on that account its cause, . . ." (*Philosophical Investigations*, tr. G.E.M. Anscombe [New York: Macmillan, 1953], p. 135[e]).

object toward which the sensation is directed. But if I speak of my hatred as hatred of the Yemenites, I am not revealing a cause of the hatred, but referring to its target.

The tentative conclusion that may be extracted from the foregoing discussion is that intentionality is characteristic of those states of a person that are expressible and absent from those that are not. If this conclusion survives further analysis, it should establish an important criterion for distinguishing the expressible from the inexpressible.

2 | I HAVE ARGUED that we do not (cannot, in fact) express sensations or perceptions, and I have contended that intentionality is a necessary condition for expression. If this contention is correct, it should contribute significantly to a deeper understanding of the concept of expression, and it will be appropriate if we can support this contention with some further theoretical scaffolding.

The first point of theoretical importance emerges from a consideration of actions. Actions are typically undertaken in accordance with our beliefs, attitudes, and desires. The expression of a desire may be an action undertaken to satisfy or fulfill that desire; and the expression of a belief or an attitude may be an action undertaken *in* the belief that something is the case, or in conformity *with* the attitude. I shall speak of these as actions undertaken *in accordance* with the relevant conditions. In each case the action bears a specifiable relation to the objects of the belief, the attitude, or the desire. There is no comparable sense in which we act in accordance with our objectless sensations.

17

One way in which we commonly identify actions as actions under a given description is to observe the relation of the behavior to the objects at, for, against, toward, or from which it is directed. Thus, a link is established between states expressed in actions and the objects of those states. I cannot express tenderness, pity, or respect without directing my behavior in some appropriate way toward their respective objects, and, conversely, the objects of my feelings are disclosed by my actions. (This is even more evident in verbal expressions than in nonverbal behavior, since the verbal expression frequently contains and often necessitates a direct reference to the object.)

That we can act in accordance with our desires and beliefs provides us with a common means of identifying the objects of those states. But there are several ways to be misled by this, and unless the notion of an object is clarified we shall be guilty of more than one variety of confusion. There are at least three important senses in which the term 'object' may be used in describing the following example. Suppose I am angry. I strike out at my wife, apologize the following day and tell her it is really the dentist I am angry with, then discover at the next session with my analyst that my father is somehow the hidden target of my feelings. There are several things to be distinguished here: (1) the object of my expressive behavior (the object toward which I direct my anger); (2) the object that I believe or *take* to be the target of my feelings; and (3) the object which is offered as the 'real' or ultimate, if not the immediate object of my anger. Let us refer to these as the immediate, virtual, and latent objects of my anger.

Now, we are concerned to elucidate the notion of an *intentional* object and its relation to expression and action; and an intentional object, as explained above, is an object given under a certain description.[8] If *A* is in a state, say, of anger, then the intentional object must be the object of his anger as given under a description which *A* himself would offer or accept. In the example above, the intentional object corresponds to the virtual object (at least during the time prior to the analytic revelation). If I *believe* that I am angry with the dentist, presumably in a description of my anger I would cite him as the object.

It is possible of course that all three objects should coincide, but wherever they do not, we are open to errors in both behavior and belief. If the intentional and immediate objects of my anger fail to coincide, then I am guilty of a misplaced expression (attacking my wife when I believe it is really the dentist I am angry with). And if the intentional and latent objects fail to coincide, I am guilty of a mistaken belief (in not realizing that it is really my father I am angry with).[9]

Now, since intentional and immediate objects need not

[8] Also, on this point, see Anthony Kenny, *Action, Emotion and Will* (New York: Humanities Press, 1963), and Brentano, *The True and the Evident*.

[9] It is sometimes argued that being mistaken about the object of my desires or my feelings (e.g. being mistaken about what it is that I *really* want) is a question of being deceived, or self-deceived as to the intentional object of my desire. But I cannot see how it is possible to be deceived about what I believe or take to be the object of my feelings; and in any event the distinction between intentional (or virtual) and latent objects should cover this possibility without requiring that we use 'intentional object' in an equivocal way.

coincide, mere observation of an action will not always reveal the identity of the intentional object. (You would have been misled in believing I was expressing anger *with* my wife, even though it is apparent that I was directing my anger *at* her.) But it is significant that the existence of some intentional object can be assumed whenever a condition of an agent is expressed in an action. It is appropriate, that is, that the agent should be able to provide an account of his action which includes a description of whatever he takes to be the object of his desire, his frustration, or his anger.

It is always possible then, in theory, to locate the intentional object of a state or condition expressed in an action, even where observation of the action does not itself disclose the object, or where the action indicates the wrong object through misplaced expression. And again the possibility of acting in *accordance* with our desires and beliefs suggests that there are often observable links between states expressed in action and their intentional objects. And wherever at least the intentional and immediate objects are identical, we have a paradigm example of behavioral expression.

Expression is not exhausted in action, however; we must also take account of the forms of involuntary behavior which count as expressions. More precisely, we shall need to consider the role of intentional objects in involuntary expressions if we are to sustain the thesis that intentionality is a necessary condition for expression.

If voluntary expressions are exemplified in actions directed in varying ways *toward* their objects, involuntary expressions occur, characteristically, as reactions *to* their intentional objects. My stammer and blush of embarrassment over my inept performance at the piano is an expressive, and involuntary, reaction to a situation in which I am ashamed of my failure. That the performance, or rather the *bad* performance is the intentional object of my embarrassment is evident if we consider that I will be embarrassed so long as I continue to believe the performance to have been inadequate. And this belief may persist independently of whether the performance was in fact inadequate, or of what others might have thought of it.

Corresponding intentional objects can be found whenever there is an occurrence of involuntarily expressive behavior. An involuntary expression of fear, shame, anger, or disgust is a *re*action—in some sense of that word—to the intentional object of the expressed state.

There is some parity then between voluntary and involuntary expressions. Both entail the presence of intentional objects, though the relation of the expression to the object is action *toward* in one case and reaction *to* in the other.

ANOTHER issue of considerable theoretical importance hinges on a grammatical possibility. Consider a situation in which a young child is crying over the loss of a doll because it was one given to her by her father. We can distinguish immediately several relevant features of the situation. There is the expression of grief (the crying), the intentional object of the grief (the lost doll), and the "cause" of the grief (the complex of relations between the child, her father, and the doll). Whether this scheme will survive intensive analysis is not at issue here. Of more immediate concern is the possibility of raising two importantly distinct questions about the expressive behavior. First, we may ask what the behavior is expressive *of* (i.e. whether the crying is an expression of grief, joy, hunger, or what). And secondly, we may ask what the expressive behavior is *about* (seeing the child crying I might reasonably ask, 'What is she crying about?'). And clearly an answer to the first question is not also an answer to the second. The questions belong to different categories. The child's crying is an expression *of* grief, but she is crying about or over the loss of the doll. The first question is a request for a description of the state expressed in the behavior. But the second, asking what the behavior is *about*, is a request for a description of the intentional object of the expressed state. If I know that someone is shouting in anger, I know the answer to the first question, but if I go on to ask, "What is he shouting about?" I shall expect a description of the object of his anger (*intentional* object, because I shall usually expect a description of something which *he*, at least, takes to be the object of his anger).

That we can ask the second of these questions implies the existence of intentional objects; and we can, I believe, ask both questions meaningfully of any instance of expressive behavior. It would be possible then, though somewhat awkward, to talk of the *aboutness* of expressive behavior in referring to its intentional character. It might be objected here that while we can ask what an expression is an expression of, we cannot ask what it is an expression about. But this misses the point, for it is the behavior under its description as *behavior* (crying, shouting, etc.) and not under its description as an expression that constitutes the referent of ϕ in both "What is the ϕ expressive of?" and "What is the ϕ about?" Both questions refer to the behavior under the same description, and consequently no equivocation is involved. This characteristic, which I shall call the "aboutness" of expressive behavior, further augments the argument that intentionality is inseparable from expression.

3 | I HAVE ARGUED that we do not, and cannot, express sensations. But the apparently decisive objection to this will have been obvious to many. Pain is a sensation, and we express pain. Therefore there is at least one sensation that we can and do express. This, as it stands, would seem to be a decisive counter-example to my contention that sensations are inexpressible, and hence fatal to the argument that intentionality is a requisite condition for the occurrence of an expression. The example, however, is not decisive, and as it stands it is merely equivocal. To clarify the problem we shall need to make a brief excursion into the psychological and neurological literature on pain.

There are, according to Hebb[10] and Morgan,[11] two general theories of pain.

In one, pain is not a special sensory mode but an effect of overstimulation of receptors for heat, cold, or pressure. In the other, pain is a sensory mode with its special receptors, pe-

[10] Hebb, *The Organization of Behavior.*
[11] C. T. Morgan, *Physiological Psychology* (New York: Mc-Graw-Hill, 1943).

ripheral nerve fibers, and conduction paths in the spinal cord. Each of these theories has its difficulties; each has something to recommend it. The two seem to have been thought of as mutually incompatible, and exhaustive: if one is proved wrong, the other must be right.[12]

Against the peripheral-intensity theory, Hebb cites evidence for the existence of pain spots in the skin, where a weak stimulation is capable of arousing pain, although a stronger stimulation in other areas does not. "Pain seems also to depend mainly on the activity of C fibers in the sensory nerve. This in itself denies that intensity is all that matters in pain."[13]

Against the theory that pain is a distinct sensory mode, Hebb points out that:

If pain is a sensory mode, it is known that its receptors must be free nerve endings, and free nerve endings are also known to mediate pressure. . . . However, very weak or very brief stimulation of pain spots or pain fibers produces no pain; as Nafe has pointed out, this has obliged supporters of the sensory-mode theory to hold that there may be "nonpainful pain."[14]

Finally, there is no specialized cortical area for pain as there is for touch, . . .[15]

The evidence from the introspective literature in psychology also appears to bear out the contention that pain may not be a coherent and discriminable sensory mode. Commenting on the experiments of Titchener,[16] Hebb remarks: "Clearly, the subjective evidence in itself does not

[12] Hebb, *The Organization of Behavior*, p. 183.
[13] *Ibid.*   [14] *Ibid.*   [15] *Ibid.*, p. 184.
[16] E. B. Titchener, "Notes from the Psychological Laboratory of Cornell University," *Am. J. Psych.*, 31 (1920), 212-14.

establish a separate modality of pain, internally unified, and distinctive from others."[17] Hebb himself proposes a fusion of the two classical theories, contending that they are not incompatible in any essential way; but he is forced to admit that the neurological evidence is inconclusive, and that his own hypothesis of the nature of pain is incomplete.

It might be argued that whatever issues are at stake among the neurologists and psychologists, pain is at least clearly different in character from an attitude or emotion; it is somehow closer to being a sensation than any other discernible part of experience. But Wolff and Hardy in their paper, "On the Nature of Pain," remark:

Views about the nature of pain have varied, but from Aristotle to relatively recent times there has been general agreement on one major issue, namely, that pain is a "passion of the soul," a feeling state, or a "quale," and not a specific sensation. Such a view was supported by thoughtful workers in nineteenth century Germany, England and America. . . . As recently as the turn of the twentieth century it was still considered debatable whether pain is indeed a sensation or exclusively a feeling reaction akin, but opposite, to that of pleasure.[18]

Wolff and Hardy are advocates of the sensory-mode theory; and yet in their conclusions they return to the question of the intimate association of pain with feeling states or "quales."

[17] Hebb, *The Organization of Behavior*, p. 187.
[18] Harold G. Wolff and J. D. Hardy, *Physiological Review*, 27 (April 1947), 167.

The distinction between perception and reaction is apparent and is easily appreciated in the case of heat, light, touch, cold and olfactory perception where the responses are not stereotyped. But when, as in the case of pain, there is an inborn as well as acquired stereotypy the contrast between perception and reaction is blurred. The reaction pattern of the organism to noxious stimuli involving pain has many components. It includes "feeling" or emotional reactions, smooth muscle, gland or skeletal muscle effects, and assumes the form of withdrawal, flight or fight.[19]

In concluding these considerations, concepts concerning pain may be touched upon again. Until the end of the nineteenth century pain was considered to be exclusively a feeling state. Later, with the discovery of special anatomic equipment and mechanisms, interest was focused on the perceptual aspects of pain. It then became clear that pain is a specific sensation, *and yet, because of its intimate linkage with strong feelings and other reaction patterns, the latter may be dominant in the experience. . . . Thus recent evidence supports the old view that the "quale" or feeling state is, to the one who suffers, perhaps the most relevant aspect of pain* [italics added].[20]

This is a crucial admission, for, if the evidence not only tends to confirm the theory that pain is a specific sensation, but also supports the classical view "that the 'quale' or feeling state is, to the one who suffers, perhaps the most relevant aspect of pain," then we should be able to meet the original objection. We can now admit that there may be a specific class of sensations called 'pain,' and that there are natural and recognizable expressions of pain, and still deny that when we "express pain" we are expressing a

[19] *Ibid.*, pp. 192-93.   [20] *Ibid.*, p. 194.

sensation. If the "dominant" and "most relevant" aspect of pain as *experienced* is a feeling state, "quale" or emotional reaction, then it should not be difficult to see that this is what is being expressed, and not the sensation itself. Expressions of pain are like expressions of distress, discomfort, dislike, and distaste; and like them, as expressions of "feeling states" or attitudes they are intentional. The *object* of an expression of pain is the sensation itself. But *what* is expressed is an attitude or feeling having the sensation as its object.

If this conclusion is rejected, then the argument must rest with those who would still insist that an expression of pain is an expression, purely and simply, of sensation. It is then their task to show how it is possible to express this sensation alone, to explain why it seems futile to speak of the expression of other sensations, and to discover the relevant difference between pain and pressure or heat as sensations that enables us to express one and not the others.

It should be apparent by now that pain is a phenomenologically complex experience, unlike the mere sensing of pressure or heat, of throbs, tickles, and pulsings, and that it encompasses an irreducible dimension of "feeling" or emotional response which, I have argued, is the condition that is articulated in expression.

4 | I HAVE ARGUED that intentionality is at least a necessary condition for expression. It remains now to explore some of the consequences of this position.

The concept of expression is associated in a primitive

way with the image of "pressing out."[21] There is something "inside" which is ex-pressed, forced out, and which in turn reveals what remains inside. But human expression is revealing in a dual sense. If we hear an outburst of nervous laughter *as* an expression of embarrassment we are aware both that something is occurring "inside" the person, and that there is some event or situation, real or imagined, by which he is embarrassed. Thus an expression points simultaneously in two directions, back toward the person and outward toward the object.[22] It is a characteristic of the concept of expression to make implicit allusion to both these features of a total situation; and for this reason it is logically incomplete to speak, for example, of the 'expression of fear,' or the 'expression of desire.' Until the object of the fear or the desire is disclosed, the description is either vacuous or chronically vague. Expression of the fear of spiders may have little in common with expression of the fear of Communism; and expression of a desire for recognition little in common with expression of a desire for oblivion.

Consequently it would be misleading to analyse expres-

---

[21] The OED gives the following etymology for the verb 'express': ". . . f. L. *ex*-out + *pressāre* to press. Taken as Eng. repr. of L. *exprimĕre* of which the chief senses were I. to press out. . . ." See also, definition II, 7: "To manifest or reveal by external tokens. Of actions, appearances, etc.: Now almost exclusively with reference to feelings or personal qualities, the wider use being arch. or poet."

[22] The object of course need not be immediately or observably present. But an expression implies the existence of some such object. I cannot be embarrassed and not be embarrassed *by* something, real or imagined, present or absent, occurrent or past.

sion as a simple two-term relation, implying that X expresses Y if X is, say, some pattern of behavior and Y some mental state or process characteristically manifested in behavior of the type of which X is a member. This suggests that the analysis is complete when it has shown how the expressive behavior reveals or refers back to the condition of the person himself. And this is equivalent to assuming, a priori, that all expressions of fear (or desire or belief) *must* have something in common, and that we are sufficiently enlightened when we know that something is an expression of fear *simpliciter*. Knowing the object of the fear would then be an interesting, though inessential addition to our knowledge. But this would be to rest content with a logically incomplete description. We cannot make sense of the notion of an expression unless we are willing to fuse this reflexive revelation with the indication of intentional objects in our analysis of the meaning of expressive behavior. An adequate analysis of the logic of 'expression' then must include a reference to the intentional character of the expressed condition.

5 | AMONG OTHER requirements for an adequate analysis of the concept of expression, we should expect that it would enable us to distinguish between expressions and other indicative relations such as signs and symptoms. It may not be immediately evident that these relations *can* be distinguished, since 'sign' and 'expression' are occasionally employed interchangeably (nervous laughter, for example, may be called a sign as well as an expression of embarrassment). But there are other occasions where the

disparity between a sign and an expression is clearly evident. Breaking out in a rash is a sign of the measles, but it is not an expression of them. More generally, there are signs, but no expressions of nonintentional states. Measles can be signified though not expressed because they are not and cannot become an intentional state of a person. We can be aware *of* them, but they are not, like beliefs and desires, of the right logical type to attain expression. Spots are a sign of the measles simply because they are the symptomatic indication of a particular nonintentional state.

Now, if expressions are always expressions of intentional states, as I have argued, it would follow that wherever 'sign' and 'expression' are both applicable we are confronted with signs of intentional states. And this would explain why some behavioral manifestations of our fears, loves, and envies are referred to alternatively as signs or expressions. But aside from instances where both terms are applicable, there are many revelations of intentional states which cannot adequately be described as signs of those states. Voluntary and object-directed actions are more naturally thought of as expressions than as signs; thus, for example, we prefer to speak of tenderness and gentleness as expressions rather than as signs of love. Conversely, involuntary and reactive expressions of intentional states are frequently referred to as signs of those states.

Moreover, were we to speak of the *signs* of such states as desire or intention we should imply that we were aware only of something contingently connected with the antecedent conditions of behavior. But clearly our intentions and desires are noncontingently connected with the behavioral patterns associated with them. We cannot describe our intentions in such a way that they are identifiable independently of the actions that would be undertaken to implement them; and the fact that intentions are thus noncontingently related to behavior explains why we choose to speak of their expressions rather than their signs. If the relation between action and intention were merely the conjectured correlation of independent events, then the pairing of sign and significandum could be invoked, indicating that certain observable features of the action signified the presence of an (unobservable) intention. But since the description of the intention is parasitic on the description of the action, no such independence can be established. And since it is characteristic of the sign relation that sign and significandum be independently describable, we cannot, given the present sense of 'intention,' talk about its signs. Similar remarks apply to desire as well, though here there are exceptions. We do speak of the signs of sexual desire, for instance. But these exceptions arise only where we are not concerned to characterize the object-directedness of the behavior, but only to indicate that the individual is in a certain state.

Now, unlike the relation between sign and significandum, the relation between an expression and the condition expressed *may* be noncontingent.[23] It is important to

[23] Cf. Austin's discussion in "Other Minds," *Philosophical Papers*, eds. J. O. Urmson and G. J. Warnock (Oxford: Clarendon, 1961). Austin argues that the expressions of anger are noncontingently related to the state of being angry. See also Ch. II.

emphasize, however, that this is not a necessary condition for all expressions, though it is probably what is implied by talking of the "natural" expressions of certain states. In any case, wherever the relation *is* noncontingent, description of the behavior as an expression cannot be given independently of the description of the condition that is expressed. Part of what we mean by 'desire' is the disposition to act in particular ways, and such actions are expressions of the desire. Hence part of what we mean by 'desire' is the disposition to initiate appropriately expressive behavior. Clearly then if this is the case, the relation between a desire and its behavioral expression is noncontingent, and any description of the behavior which presents it *as* an expression is, to that extent, a function of the description of the desire. Thus a description of behavior as expressive of a particular desire is also a partial description of the desire.

This should help to explain, finally, why actions *express*, rather than *signify*, intentions and desires. The concept of a sign is inadequate to describe a relation, such as that between intention and action or desire and action in which the terms are noncontingently connected. 'Expression' is the only logically adequate term that we possess for indicating a complex in which object-directed action and a noncontingently related condition of the agent are present.

To summarize then, the concept of intentionality, conjoined with those of action and contingency, should enable us to map significant areas of coincidence and divergence between signs and expressions, and this strengthens the case for choosing intentionality as a focal point in our analysis of expression.

6 | ONE FURTHER objection to the claim that intentionality is a necessary condition for expression may be anticipated here. It is intelligible to speak of the expression of such states as anxiety and depression, and yet these states are frequently said to lack objects in the sense in which it is appropriate to speak of the objects of fear, hope, and affection. Anxiety, for instance, has been called a form of "objectless fear." And depression, as Ducasse remarks, remains qualitatively the same whether caused by objective difficulties in one's way or by "obscure unconscious physiological causes."

In short, the plain fact, as distinguished from theories, is that emotions, feelings, and moods, in a large proportion of their occurrences do well-up in us spontaneously from the unconscious workings of body and soul, and not at all in response to an objective situation.[24]

Ducasse apparently takes this to mean that, since emotions and moods may have their genesis in unconscious physiological processes, as alcohol may generate enthusiasm, the question of the objects of these states need not arise. Feelings or moods which are induced in this way are not responses to objective situations and we cannot therefore speak of them being "called out by objects." But it is not clear that this does prohibit us from raising questions

[24] C. J. Ducasse, *The Philosophy of Art* (New York: Dover, 1966), pp. 92-93.

concerning the objects of such states. The manner in which a feeling or an emotional state is generated or "called out" tells us nothing about the existence or nonexistence of an object of that state. Alcoholically induced elation may still be elation *over* something—something trivial perhaps, or something which in a more sober moment would be regarded with less enthusiasm, but which can nevertheless be spoken of as the intentional object of the present feeling. And narcotically induced euphoria is not objectless merely because its origin is organic and not "psychological." The psychedelic subject is still fascinated *by* the color of the room or absorbed *in* the sound of the rain.

Anthony Kenny notes that emotions which are often described as objectless are not so in fact.

We are often unaccountably depressed, on days when for no reason everything seems black; but pointless depression is not objectless depression, and the objects of depression are the things which seem black.[25]

And even Freud ultimately adopted the view that anxiety (*angst*) is not fear of nothing, but rather a fear of something, albeit *Je ne sais quoi.*[26]

It is at least consistent and plausible to maintain that the objects of anxiety are elusive not because they are nonexistent, but because 'anxiety' describes the condition of being afraid where the object of the fear is either unknown, unrecognized, or repressed, or where it is simply too diffuse to be easily located or precisely described. Per-

[25] Kenny, *Action, Emotion and Will*, pp. 60-61.
[26] *Beyond the Pleasure Principle*, Collected Works, Vol. xviii (London: Hogarth, 1953).

vasive moods and all-encompassing attitudes (*Weltanschauungen*) suffer from this form of imprecision, and yet it may be more reasonable to say that such states have diffuse or indeterminate objects rather than to insist that they have none at all. That my moods cast a shadow over everything I encounter does not prove that they cast no shadow at all.

If it seems inappropriate or odd at times to ask for the objects of moods, depressions, and anxieties, the oddness may arise not from requesting a description of a nonexistent object, but from the difficulty of adequately describing objects which are either unknown, only vaguely discerned, indeterminate, or diffuse. That "a man may be paralysed by a conviction of impending doom, though he can give no account of what he dreads"[27] does not entitle us to reason that his inability to give such an account is proof of the absence of an object of his dread. Of course it is not proof of its presence either, but to speak of objects which are undetected, unrecognized, indeterminate, or diffuse is at least a reasonable alternative to selecting a few human feelings as peculiarly "objectless." And this way of speaking of them has the advantage of being consistent with our conception of more determinate, object-oriented states, rather than constituting an exception to that view, as is the case with the rival account. Finally then, there seems to be no conclusive reason for regarding the objection—that we commonly express "objectless" states such as anxiety and depression—as a decisive counter-example to the thesis that intentionality is necessary to expression.

[27] Kenny, p. 61.

CHAPTER **II** INFERENCE AND EXPRESSION

II

I | HAVING ESTABLISHED a criterion for determining which states of a person are expressible in behavior, we may now consider the logical relations that link behavioral expressions and those states of a person that are said to be expressed. Before undertaking a discussion of these relations, however, we must note an important distinction marked by a difference in syntactic form.

Consider the following sentences:

S_1 A sad expression is a mark of the thoroughbred beagle.

S_2 An expression of sadness crossed her face as she watched him close the gate.

'Sad expression' does not mean 'expression of sadness'; but this is easily overlooked wherever they can be interchanged without apparent loss or alteration of meaning, as in S_2 above. The difference is more evident if we attempt the substitution in sentences whose subjects denote insensate objects. Noh masks and cypress trees may *have* sad expressions, but their expressions are not expressions *of* sadness. Sad expressions are to the expression of sadness as anger-like behavior is to the expression of anger. Anger-like behavior may occur in the absence of anger, but an expression of anger cannot (*logically* cannot); and analogously, sad expressions may occur without sadness (the beagle and the Noh mask), while the expression of sadness cannot.

Moreover, the syntactic arrangement cannot in many cases be shuffled at all. There are sneering expressions, but

39

there are no expressions of sneer. A sneering expression may well *be* expressive of something—contempt or disdain perhaps—but we cannot discover what it expresses by a simple syntactic maneuver, translating 'ϕ expression' into 'expression of ϕ'; and even where there are symmetrical syntactic possibilities—that is, where 'ϕ expression' and 'expression of ϕ' are both available—a particular occurrence of a ϕ expression need not be an expression *of ϕ*. We shall see on reflection that constructions which exemplify these two syntactic forms are logically independent.

The outlines of this distinction can be sketched briefly. Wherever the qualifier appears before the noun ('ϕ expression') the phrase (A) is a *description* of certain observable features of a situation; and whenever the form 'expression of ϕ' (B) occurs, it may commonly be taken to be an inference warranting expression, relating some intentional state of a person to particular aspects of his observable behavior. Since the larger part of this study is concerned with an analysis of expressions which exemplify syntactic form B, the possibility of confusion or inconsistency can be lessened if this distinction is kept in mind. An analysis of syntactic form A presents no problems apart from those of any systematic study of descriptive discourse, and that is not the present objective.[1]

Still, there is one point that remains unsettled. There must be some connection, it would seem, between sad expressions and the expression of sadness, even if sneering

[1] We shall return to this issue in Chs. IV and V where it is relevant to the discussion of art and expression.

expressions are not so related to expressions of sneer-(ness). It cannot be mere coincidence that some objectively discernible features of the world also happen to be connected with the expression of certain states of mind and character. This much may be admitted, but I would argue that the connection is genetic and not logical.[2] Innumerable expressions of human sadness have deposited a calcified and conventional image of sadness—the human figure, heavy, bent, and slow, with slackened mouth and downcast eyes. And around this conventional image the descriptive content of 'sad expression' has crystallized.

Without such conventions no consistent descriptive meaning could be attached to any instance of a ϕ expression, and the existence of accessible conventions of this sort explains, in part, our ability to "project" sadness, anger, and despair into the nonhuman world. But we must be careful to notice the dissociation of the two syntactic forms at just this point. The convention enables us to describe a set of features as a 'ϕ expression' *without implication*. A malformed face may bear an unmistakably cruel expression; but, having perceived this, nothing further can be inferred about its owner's inclination to cruelty. By contrast, to speak of an expression *of* cruelty in a face *is* to license such implications.

Conventional expectations are not as binding for in-

---

[2] The relation discussed here is not that between *sadness* and the expression of sadness but the relation between sad expressions and the expression of sadness. The former *is* a logical relation, in the sense that it is noncontingent (see Section 2 of this chapter).

stances of B as they are for instances of A, and we may evolve novel or even bizarre ways of expressing some of our intentional states. (One need only recall some of the classical examples of aberrant behavior in psychoanalytic literature.) The very possibility of novel expressions depends on the absence of restrictive conventions, or, more commonly, on the open-textured character of existing conventions. Such possibilities are not open equally to instances of A. The descriptive content of 'sad expression' must remain relatively fixed within a given linguistic and cultural setting, or risk distortion which would deprive it of any useful function.

Because of these asymmetries there is no logically binding link between A and B such that one is inferrible from the other. Membership in A neither entails nor rules out membership in B; they are logically independent. If it is an error to believe that the presence of a sad expression invariably betrays an expression of sadness, then it is equally erroneous to think that an expression of sadness will invariably present us with something describable as a sad expression. Sad expressions do not entail, nor are they entailed by expressions of sadness, though they are related in other ways; and there are numerous instances of both A and B which cannot be transformed into meaningful or parallel instances of the other (e.g. sneering expressions and expressions of intention).

Before undertaking the discussion which follows, I must emphasize that I shall not be concerned with the psychological or practical difficulties involved in recognizing an expression, but rather with the logical and inferential relations that are implied in *calling* something an expression. Accordingly, the logic of 'expression' (*B*) may be outlined schematically as follows:

If *A*'s behavior *B* is an *expression of X*, then there is a warrantable inference from *B* to an intentional state of *A*, such that it would be true to say that *A* has (or is in state) *S*; and where *S* and *X* are identical.

In the remaining sections of this chapter, I shall illustrate and defend this scheme, and finally, I shall attempt to indicate how it may serve to distinguish expressing from such related activities as acting, imitating, and pretending.

2 | BEHAVIOR, as Carnap has observed,[3] is expressive if it discloses something about the *person* exhibiting the behavior. A mincing walk, a timorous voice, a seductive gesture are expressive when they reveal something of the person himself, and the conclusions of the previous chapter suggest that what is revealed in expressive behavior are intentional states of the person.[4]

Now it is clear that our intentional states are not always voluntarily displayed, and that often the most familiar of human expressions are involuntarily engendered. Loss of

[3] Rudolph Carnap, *Philosophy and Logical Syntax* (London: Kegan Paul, Trench, Trubner, 1935).

[4] Here, and throughout this chapter, 'expressive behavior' is to be understood to imply that the behavior is *an expression (B)* of something. In Ch. IV we shall have reason to distinguish this interpretation from a noninferential sense of 'expressive behavior.'

43

muscular control and vocal constriction in fear, blushing in embarrassment are, for example, largely involuntary. Their involuntariness in fact guarantees their consistency as recognizable expressions. Accordingly, we have the following grammatical forms to mark this distinction: 'A expressed his f for x by ϕ-ing' and 'A's ϕ-ing expressed his f for x.' To say of a person that *he* expressed his abhorrence of the goat cheese by grimacing differs from saying that his grimacing at the sight of the cheese was an expression of his abhorrence. The behavior reveals, in either case, the same intentional state, though in the first case the implication is that the behavior was voluntary or deliberate, and in the second, that it was not. It will be important in what follows to keep this distinction in mind, since the relation of a person's expressive behavior to the intentional states that it reveals will vary to some extent with the shift from one grammatical form to the other.

We may now go on to explore the relation between expressive behavior and those intentional states of a person that are revealed, displayed, or, in some way shown forth in his behavior; and I shall argue that there is no descriptively distinct class of performances or bodily movements that constitutes expressive behavior. The concept of an expression implies the warranting of certain inferential structures, and it cannot be located by scrutiny of the descriptions of behavior alone, unless those descriptions include among their truth conditions the relevant inferential moves. Explosive laughter, a facial grimace, a shudder, or a periodic tic are, in themselves, neither expressive nor nonexpressive, and only if we have reason to connect the behavior inferentially with some desire, belief, intent, or conflict are we entitled to treat it as an expression.

It will be useful at this point then to examine some of the logical features of the inferential relations warranted by behavioral expressions.[5]

If an acquaintance who is afflicted with a spasmodic tic is a victim of no organic failure, but a despondent and chronically repressed individual whose emotional difficulties are directly related to the appearance of his tic, we may have good reason to believe that his tic is an expression of his emotional state. And the inferential connection here is straightforwardly Humean. Cause and effect are independently describable and constantly conjoined. The only qualification to be added is that the "cause" is psychological and not physical. This can be stated as a general requirement of all inferences of this type, since there would be no evidence of the presence of an *intentional* state if the cause were organic, and the behavior would then be nonexpressive.

It is clear then that calling the movement a 'tic' is not by itself sufficient to indicate whether it is or is not an expression. There are cases, however, where our description of a person's behavior or his appearance is not "neutral" in this respect, and our choice of words may often indicate the kind of inferential move that we consider the description to warrant. Consider, for example, the following descriptions of a person at a particular time, t-1:

[5] Reference to a warranted inference here must not be thought to indicate the psychological process of *making* an inference. It is intended rather to indicate the presence of certain relations that are implied by the use of 'expression' (B).

D_1 A has a red face.
D_2 A's face is flushed.
D_3 A is blushing.

To describe A as having a red face does not necessarily imply a relation between the color of his face and a correlated psychological state. There are people who have naturally ruddy complexions, and there is nothing in D_1 which suggests that A is not such a case. D_2, on the other hand, would seem to imply that at least a change in A's complexion has occurred, but it is still neutral as to its cause. D_3, however, would be out of place if we were not willing to admit a connection between the color of A's face and some psychological state such as embarrassment or shame.

There are descriptions then which can be used correctly only where a relation between observed appearance and a psychological state of the person is thought to exist. To use D_3 rather than D_1 or D_2 is to imply that the appearance of a red face can be linked inferentially to some psychological state and thus may constitute an expression of that state.

The truth conditions for saying that A is blushing are logically related to the truth conditions for saying that A's appearance is an expression of his embarrassment or shame. Consider how such a description might be falsified. If we were to discover that A had been eating hot peppers or drinking heavily, for example, we might be led to retract D_3 and replace it with a more neutral description such as D_1 or D_2. Descriptions such as D_3 carry with them *intentional implications*, i.e. they provide conceptual linkages between observable features of the world and intentional states of persons.

The suggestion that there are conceptual as well as causal linkages to be considered here leads us to the next, and more significant point. There is a (now familiar) argument in philosophy that psychological predicates occupy a crucial and pivotal position in our language. They range, according to this view,[6] over both public and private domains, and they refer not to the covert mental life alone but to a complex of inner agitation and outer show. 'Anger,' 'jealousy,' and 'depression' acquire their meanings from a coalescence of the public and the private. Thus jealous behavior is not merely *evidence* for the presence of jealousy but, in an important sense, a constituent part of the complex referent of the predicate 'jealous.'[7]

True, the jealous husband may conceal his jealousy so artfully as to avoid discovery, but he will need to make an

[6] Differing versions of the position which I shall schematically outline above may be found in: Kenny, *Action, Emotion and Will*; P. F. Strawson, *Individuals* Ch. III (New York: Doubleday, 1963); Austin, "Other Minds."

[7] Cf. Strawson's remark that "X's depression *is* something, one and the same thing, which is felt, but not observed, by X, and observed, but not felt, by others than X" (*Individuals*, p. 105), and Austin's observation that "It seems fair to say that 'being angry' is in many respects like 'having mumps.' It is a description of a whole pattern of events, including occasion, symptoms, feeling and manifestation, and possibly other factors besides. . . . Moreover, it is our confidence in the general pattern that makes us apt to say we 'know' another man is angry when we have only observed parts of the pattern: for the parts of the pattern are related to each other very much more intimately than, for example, newspaper men scurrying in Brighton are related to a fire in Fleet Street" (Austin, "Other Minds," pp. 77-78).

effort to prevent detection. He will need to repress or disguise the inclinations to act which would normally accompany his feelings. On the other hand, we should feel justified in accusing a man of jealousy, in spite of his protestations, if his behavior were sufficiently obvious (if, for instance, he consistently kept his wife from contact with younger men, followed her about at parties, and hired detectives to watch her in his absence), and we should feel entitled to call such a man jealous even in the face of his (sincere) disavowal of any conscious awareness or feeling of jealousy.[8] And if this is the case with jealousy, we might expect that other psychological predicates will behave in a similar manner, that their import will be neither univocally mental nor behavioristic, neither scandalously public nor surreptitiously private.

This position is by now well entrenched and widely accepted. It is reviewed here, without further defense, to bring out the implications for our analysis of expression. Behavior that is expressive of jealousy (or anger or depression) is a *constituent part* of that state on this view, and consequently, I would argue, the inference which proceeds from the behavior to the expressed state is not a causal inference but one which moves from a part of a conceptual complex to another part, or to the whole of it. We are close here to the grammarian's category of *synecdoche*. A mast is not merely evidence of the presence of an approaching ship; it is a part of the ship. It "stands for" the ship as part to whole, not as effect to cause or sign to

[8] Cf. Errol Bedford, "Emotions," *Proceedings of the Aristotelian Society*, LVII (1956-57), 281-304.

significandum. And so with expressive behavior. Jealous behavior is not *merely* evidence of the presence of jealousy; it is a part of the complex pattern which comprises the full significance of 'jealousy.' There may be jealousy without jealous behavior, of course, just as there may be ships without masts, but this does not mean that the behavior, when present, is not a proper and logical constituent of the jealousy, any more than it means that masts, when present, are not proper parts of the ship.

In applying psychological predicates like 'anger' and 'jealousy' we employ an imprecisely extended range of criteria, none of which are necessary, but many of which are sufficient for their application. This is evidenced by our willingness to predicate such states as jealousy both on the basis of behavior alone and in the absence of any introspected awareness of jealous feelings, and equally, at other times, on the basis of such feelings alone and in the absence of symptomatic behavior. Criteria for the application of such concepts are heterogeneous and complementary. Taken singly they are not necessary, though they may be sufficient conditions, but only taken collectively do they comprise the full *sense* of the conceptual complex.

It might be argued that the propriety of inference is challenged if behavior alone can justify the ascription of such predicates as 'jealous' or 'depressed,' since there should then be no room for an inference from the behavior to something else. But even assuming we are entitled to *predicate* 'jealous' on the basis of overt behavior alone, we invariably *intend* more than a summary description of the observable behavior in making such predications. We intend to attribute to the person, in addition to his behavior, some associated set of attitudes, tendencies, beliefs, feelings, or motives, conscious or otherwise. (We need to be reminded here that the meaning of a term and the criteria for its application need not be identical.)

This incidentally suggests a resolution of the antinomy that 1) We can *see* anger, depression, and jealousy in a gesture, a bodily attitude, or a face; and 2) It is impossible to observe anger or depression directly; their presence can only be *inferred* from their external expressions. If the relation between these states and their expressions is analogous to the rhetorical relation of synecdoche, as I have suggested, then it should be possible to avoid the contradiction implied by the antinomy.

The appearance of a mast on the horizon usually justifies the claim that a ship has been sighted, and the objection that the ship has not been *directly* observed but merely inferred from something else is misguided, since it is a *part* of the ship that has been sighted. However, the objection is relevant insofar as it asserts that an inference is entailed in referring to a whole on the strength of the observation of a part. The mistake, concealed in the antinomy, is to regard the expression of intentional states such as jealousy as external indices of inner happenings, as public events contingently related to private occurrences, rather than as constituent parts of a complex occurrence. Obviously, we can *see* jealousy in a man's behavior, if that behavior is itself a constituent in the referent of 'jealousy'; and just as obviously, we cannot *directly* observe a man's jealousy if we *now* mean by 'jealousy' the whole of the ref-

50

erential complex including the essentially private feelings and sensations, or if we *now* mean by 'jealousy' those feelings and sensations alone. The antinomy is generated only when we attempt to restrict the reference of psychological predicates of this type to wholly private or to exclusively public occurrences.

When we speak of the 'expression of jealousy' then, we imply the validity of an inferential move from one segment of the conceptual matrix which comprises the meaning of 'jealousy' to another segment of that matrix, or to the whole of it.

It may be hoped that, whatever flaws this analysis may have, it avoids at least the traditional difficulties of the Cartesian model which casts all inferences concerning character or mind in the form of deriving "inner" causes from "outer" effects. Expressive behavior, on the Cartesian model, is merely another instance of a physical event signaling the occurrence of an (unobservable) mental event, and we have seen how little this accords with the actual use of many psychological predicates, and how inadequately it accounts for the distinctions we have drawn between expressions and signs.

To speak of an expression then, is not to refer to a special class of observably discriminable movements, but to imply that some particular inferential pattern is warranted.

3 | I HAVE SAID that there is nothing intrinsic to behavior which marks it as unmistakably expressive—nothing, that is, which identifies it as an expression *of φ*—and that a reference to behavioral expressions implies the

existence of a relation between the behavior and an intentional state of the person to whom the behavior belongs. But there is a *surface* to expressive behavior that may become detached. The child who pretends, the actor who portrays, the mime who imitates, and the hypocrite who feigns, all attempt, in differing ways, to strip the surface of expressive behavior from the character it normally reveals; and thus it might be thought that there are activities in which one may express a feeling or an attitude that he does not have. If this were the case, the inferential relations I have claimed are implied by the use of 'expression' would be absent in some instances. But I shall argue that these activities, rather than being alternate or peripheral modes of expression, are best understood as standing in varyingly parasitic relations to expression, and that we must distinguish the genuine expression from activities that merely wear the mask of expressive behavior.

To say that an actor is expressing despair, for instance, is often to say something that is logically oblique. When Evans portrays the despair of Lear, it is *Lear's* despair and not Evans's that is expressed in the actor's gestures. The actor is distinct from the character he portrays, and the thoughts and emotions he "expresses," if he is successful, are those of the character he presents and not his own. We should say that the actor *portrays* Lear, and that it is Lear who expresses Lear's despair.

Advocates of method acting might insist that ideally the emotions of the actor and the character he portrays should be identical or qualitatively similar. In that case it would appear that the actor may be expressing, in a single action,

52

both the emotions of the character and his own. But even the joint conditions of being grief-stricken and simultaneously playing Lear are not sufficient to justify the ellipsis to 'The actor is expressing Lear's grief.' We should rather say that he is both expressing his own grief and *representing* Lear-expressing-Lear's-grief. Willingness to accept the ellipsis may be encouraged by the fact that there is only one sequence of actions in sight. But this single sequence requires two distinct descriptions just *because* it is a theatrical portrayal. There are segments of two life histories before us.[9] That they are both presented in the actions of a single person should not obscure recognition that a single action may both express *and* represent an expression, and where this does occur it argues for a division of logical subjects of the action. The actor may express himself through the role he plays, but he cannot, while expressing himself, simultaneously represent his own expression— just as one cannot both act and simultaneously *imitate* his actions, though he may act in imitation of others or in imitation of himself at other times.

The parallel with imitation is instructive. The imitation of an action requires another action, and the gap between the actions cannot be closed. Imitation is inflexibly relational, and conflation of the imitated and imitating actions would dissolve the relation. Self-imitations are possible only insofar as they relate present to previous actions of the imitator. Logically, imitating is on a par with copying and forging. And just as nothing is a copy, a forgery, or an imitation of itself, nothing is a representation of itself.

[9] It is irrelevant that one of the life histories may be fictional.

The gap between the represented and the representing is equally unbridgeable. Even self-portraits are not portraits of themselves. The actor cannot both express himself and represent his *own* expressions since the requisite relational space would be missing; and, since to act is to represent, if he is *merely* expressing himself, he cannot also be acting. Where a single action then is both an expression and a representation of an expression we should expect to find distinct logical subjects for the expressions—in this case, the actor and the character. And even though the expressions of actor and character are contingently identical, it does not follow that they are equally, or indifferently, objects of dramatic interest; just as it does not follow from the contingent identity of the Evening Star and the Morning Star that what we admire in the evening is the brilliance of the Morning Star. Contingent identity is no license for free substitution in all predicative contexts.

An understanding of these semantic restrictions on 'expression' and 'representation' should help to explain the necessity for separate though parallel descriptions of theatrical performances. Collapsing or mixing the descriptions of these separate life histories generates hybridized statements, innocent enough in the morning reviews, but profoundly misleading where we are concerned to understand the systematic complex of relations among expression and portrayal, actor and character.

Moreover, if expression were the *gauge* of successful acting, theatrical performances would be judged by determining whether the actor had succeeded in expressing himself through the role that he plays. But a performance, no matter how satisfying as an expression from the perspective of the actor, remains to be judged by its adequacy as a representation of the expressive behavior of the Lears, the Iagos, and the Lomans he portrays. Method acting may be a powerful technique for generating effective representations of expressive behavior, but it is no crutch for the theorist who would argue that successful expression is the object of our deepest theatrical interests. One who is moved by the actor's grief has lost sight of Lear.

Again, if expression were the key to successful theatrical performance it would be difficult to understand why the actor should need to study his craft, or indeed why acting should be an art or craft at all. The actor studies his own gestures, facial expressions, and vocal intonations not because he needs to infer from them what feelings *he* is expressing, but because he must determine that his actions, whatever they may express, also effectively and appropriately represent the expressions of his *dramatis personae*. And one can imagine the taciturn method actress who must *express* extreme anger to *represent* effectively the mild annoyance of Shakespeare's more volatile Katherina. Their feelings are graphed on different scales.

Finally, these observations suggest that acting is best thought of not as a species of expressive behavior but rather as an activity which appropriates the surface of expressive behavior for representational purposes. Where genuine expression does occur in the theater it is a means and not an end.

The relation of the actor to the expressive surface of behavior then is reasonably clear; but what shall we say of a child who *pretends* to be afraid? Is he also pretending to *express* fear? Or is he accomplishing the pretense by actually (really) expressing fear? Either alternative is distressing. 'Pretending to express ϕ' has no paradigmatic role in the language, contrasted with 'pretending to *be* ϕ'; and it is therefore difficult to see what would count as an instance of "pretending to express fear." The second alternative is equally unhappy. If we choose to say that the pretender is *really* expressing fear, then we shall have no way of distinguishing between 'really expressing' fear and merely going through the motions of being afraid. The second way of speaking commits us to identifying these two descriptions. And there is something strange in proposing 'He's really *expressing* fear, but he's not really afraid' as an explication of pretence.

Consider the following parallel. A sentence which is asserted when uttered on one occasion may be uttered nonassertorically on another. 'I am English' may be assertoric when uttered by Lord Russell, and nonassertoric when uttered by a Tahitian language student rehearsing a grammatical exercise. Yet we can speak intelligibly of the "same" sentence occurring on both occasions. Analogously, a behavioral pattern which expresses fear on one occasion may occur on another occasion nonexpressively. But perhaps the parallel is misleading, for we began by asking whether the behavior in pretence was *expressive* behavior, and it might be objected that the analogy has been distorted. Thus, the same sentence may be used to inform or deceive, depending on the context of utterance, but in both cases it is used assertorically. Lying depends on this: I lie by asserting something I believe to be false. The analogy would then appear to be this: the same behavioral pattern may occur on separate occasions to reveal or dissimulate character, but in both cases it is expressive behavior. Acceptance of this analogy would lead us to say that a person who pretends to be afraid is using behavior to express an emotion he knows he does not have; and, more generally, to say that expression, like assertion, is compatible with intentional dissemblance. But for a number of reasons this is a misleading analogy. Aside from skirting the complexities of pretence,[10] it thrusts back upon us all the evils of identifying expression with a discrete class of behavioral patterns isolated from whatever inferential structures they may imply. We would then be committed to say, given a description of certain gestures or facial configurations, that these patterns either were or were not expressions of a certain state, and we should be entitled to assert this in the absence of any further effort. It would be sufficient to know that a particular look had crossed a human face to claim incorrigibly that an expression of ϕ had occurred. And this claim, once established, would be immune from revision in the light of further revelations of the person's thoughts, feelings, or intentions. But the fact remains that we *are* prepared to modify or retract our imputations of expression whenever we discover that the gesture or the look was accompanied by thoughts, feelings, or intentions different from those we

[10] Cf. J. L. Austin, "Pretending," and G.E.M. Anscombe, "Pretending," *Proceedings of the Aristotelian Society*, Supplementary Volume XXXII (1958).

had supposed, or by none at all. All distinctions among imitating, pretending, acting, and expressing would dissolve if this were not so.

Our problem was to determine whether the child who pretends to be afraid is also pretending to express fear, or whether he is actually expressing fear as a means of accomplishing the pretence, and I have tried to indicate my grounds for uneasiness with both alternatives. 'He's only pretending to express fear' and 'He's really expressing fear, but he's not really afraid' leave us to choose between the meaningless and the paradoxical. The way out of this will be apparent only if we recognize the oddness of the question. The logic implicit in the use of these terms should in fact lead us to suspect that pretending and expressing are incompatible activities. 'A is expressing ϕ' implies that A is (or has) ϕ, whereas 'A is pretending to be ϕ,' implies that A is *not* ϕ. If I am pretending then, I cannot also be expressing, and if I am expressing, I cannot also be pretending. The child is neither pretending to express fear, nor "really" expressing it. He is pretending to *be* afraid, and this description bars 'expression' and its cognates from appearing on the same bill. 'Pretending' and 'expressing' are rivals for the same role, not supporting players in one another's act.

It may be objected that pretence does not exclude expression—that, e.g. my pretending to be annoyed may be an expression of my desire for attention. But we should recall that the logic of 'expression' (B) requires that S and X be identical—that if I am expressing annoyance it follows that I am annoyed—and it is just this identity that pretending precludes. No doubt I am expressing *something* when I pretend to ϕ (or to be ϕ), but I cannot, if I am pretending to ϕ, also be expressing ϕ. Pretence differs from expression just insofar as it *rules out* the identity of S and X. (We could of course *give* a sense to 'pretending to express,' but whatever assignment we might invent for it will merely duplicate the function of some established and less tortuous construction.)

Acting and pretending, along with imitating, feigning, simulating and other activities of this sort must be clearly distinguished from expressing. The "surface" of expressive behavior is easily detached and reproduced, and much of our time is taken up with such pursuits, both in play and in earnest. But nothing will be gained by assimilating such activities and by regarding them as variant forms of expression. Rather, their relation to expression is that of a class of activities which parasitically exploit the observable surface of expressive behavior for purposes which range from deceit to diversion.[11]

---

[11] Ritual or ceremonial behavior is somewhat more difficult to classify. There are ritual displays of emotional behavior in nearly all societies at the more significant *rites de passages*. The practice of *keening* at an Irish wake, for example, does not require that those who wail and moan be genuinely grief-stricken, and so, on my account, does not require an expression of grief. But neither is it clearly a case of pretence, since there is no attempt to mislead or deceive. *Keening* seems closer to acting than to expressing, pretending, or imitating; but, although acting would be a less misleading description of the practice, it is not an entirely happy one. In Ch. III, we shall have occasion to consider some of the ritual uses of language in relation to linguistic expression.

4 | WE HAVE NOW seen how both intentionality and certain forms of inferential connection are criterial conditions for the correct use of 'expression' (B). The truth conditions of 'A's behavior B is an expression of X' are such that a particular statement of this form is always false when it can be shown either (a) that there is no relation between B and some intentional state S of the person, or (b) that S and X are not identical.

If acting and pretending were also modes of expressing, these criteria would fail to mark the logical parameters of 'expression'; but I have tried to show that they are not, and that the relation of these activities to expression is logically oblique and parasitic.

CHAPTER **III** LANGUAGE AND
EXPRESSION

1 | IN A LECTURE delivered at the University of London in 1934, Rudolf Carnap made a number of remarks which, in the light of subsequent developments in philosophy, are worth quoting at some length:

Now we have analysed the propositions of metaphysics in a wide sense of this word, including not only transcendental metaphysics, but also the problems of philosophical Reality and lastly normative ethics. Perhaps many will agree that the propositions of all these kinds of metaphysics are not verifiable, i.e. that their truth cannot be examined by experience. And perhaps many will grant for this reason that they have not the character of scientific propositions. But when I say that they are without sense, assent will probably seem more difficult. Someone may object: these propositions in the metaphysical books obviously have an effect upon the reader, and sometimes a very strong effect; therefore they certainly *express* something. That is quite true, they *do* express something, but nevertheless, they have no sense, no theoretical content.

We have here to distinguish two functions of language, which we may call the expressive function and the representative function. Almost all the conscious and unconscious movements of a person, including his linguistic utterances express something of his feelings, his present mood, his temporary or permanent dispositions to reaction, and the like. Therefore we may take almost all his movements and words as symptoms from which we can infer something about his feelings or his character. That is the expressive function of movements and words. But besides that, a certain portion of linguistic utterances (e.g. "this book is black"), as distinguished from other linguistic utterances and movements, has a second function: these utterances represent a certain state of affairs; they tell us that something is so and so; they assert something, they predicate something, they judge something.

. . . .

Now many linguistic utterances are analogous to laughing in that they have only an expressive function, no representative function. Examples of this are cries like "Oh, Oh" or, on a higher level, lyrical verses. The aim of a lyrical poem in which occur the words "sunshine" and "clouds," is . . . to express certain feelings of the poet and to excite similar feelings in us. A lyrical poem has no assertional sense, no theoretical sense, it does not contain knowledge.[1]

What emerges immediately from these remarks is a conception of language in which two distinct functions are contrasted. Certain utterances (e.g. "this book is black") may both express and represent, but words or utterances which are not used to "represent," which "have no sense, no theoretical content," are purely "expressive."

However useful it might appear to have a schematic distinction of this sort, it quickly breeds more confusion than it dispels. In the absence of any attempt to discriminate among the widely diverse linguistic functions which have been grouped under 'expression,' there is a temptation to obscure differences which have great philosophical importance. In any case, it is unwise to assume that a linguistic dualism, like that of Carnap's, does more than mark the starting point of enquiry.

What is to be gained then by distinguishing between representation (or description) and expression? The choice of "function" in Carnap's account is significant. He does not say there are two sorts of language, but rather

---

[1] *Philosophy and Logical Syntax*, pp. 26-29.

two distinct linguistic functions. It is important to insist on this, since many philosophers (including Carnap himself) have written as if certain words, phrases, and syntactical structures were inherently descriptive, or inherently expressive. Thus 'the barn is red' and 'Humbug!' may be labeled respectively descriptive and expressive, even in the absence of a context of utterance. But this is misleading, and the reasons that suggest its inadequacy also call into question the validity of any theory which attempts to mark off a coherent class of purely expressive (or emotive, or performative) linguistic elements and oppose these to another class of purely descriptive elements.

Wittgenstein has suggested that utterances such as 'I am in pain' may be seen as a form of learned pain behavior, a linguistically sophisticated substitute for the more primitive and natural expression of pain.[2] Thus, in spite of the indicative syntactical form, the "statement" 'I am in pain' is functionally equivalent to the more primitive *expression* of pain. We are to infer then that 'I am in pain' *may* be merely expressive, since it replaces the natural expression and is used to do the same job. There is a similar and converse argument. Consider this case: You are asked, 'How was DeGaulle received in Algiers?' 'Boo!' you shout vigorously in response, thereby conveying as much as if you had replied: 'He was greeted with audible hostility.' Nor would we react to this response as if it were *necessarily* an outburst of feeling or merely an expression of personal antagonism. In the context of the utterance it is as natural to interpret the exclamation as a response to a

[2] *Philosophical Investigations*, paragraph 244, p. 89e.

request for information as it would be to interpret it as an expression of distaste where it spontaneously follows a bad performance of *Verklärte Nacht*.

It is often argued in support of the descriptive/expressive dichotomy that descriptions are cognitively significant and hence bearers of truth values, whereas purely expressive constructions are illegitimate candidates for that honor. But (think of the last example), if I have reason to believe that DeGaulle was received in Algiers with wild enthusiasm, I will react to your emphatic 'Boo' by objecting that that is false. It is not always absurd to ask whether a 'Boo!' or a 'Hurrah!' is true or false, for exclamations may imply, even if they do not assert propositions whose truth values are in question.[3] It has frequently been pointed out also that exclamations like 'Hurrah!' and 'Bravo!' neither name nor describe nor refer to anything. And so, it is argued, such devices must have a purely expressive role; they must, that is, be mere effusions of feeling. But these are not legitimate or necessary alternatives. Suppose that, following the duet from *Traviata*, Act IV, I shout not 'Bravo!' but 'Brava!' 'Brava!' does not refer to the soprano as, say, 'Renata' does, but it clearly *has* reference to her, and distinguishes her from the tenor as the object of my enthusiasm. If such expressions were simply effusions of feeling, the grammatical distinction would be irrelevant; and it is not.

If we are to take seriously the fashionable imperative to abandon the search for hypostatized "meanings" in favor of the concepts of "use" and "function," it should

[3] In such cases the exclamations stand as sentence surrogates.

be increasingly apparent that there are no descriptive, expressive, or performative words or sentences; there are only these employments of them. But 'red' is a predicate (or predicable) and 'Hurrah!' an exclamation, are they not? Usually; and for the grammarian intent upon labeling linguistic components that will do. Our difficulty begins where we expect the categories of classification to be invariantly concretized in distinct forms of discourse. We expect to find predicables used to represent, to describe, to pred*icate*. And this expectation is commonly gratified. It is a small thing then to endow the class of words and expressions most frequently used to predicate with the indelible property of *being* descriptive words and expressions. There are contexts, however, where exclamations such as 'Boo!' or 'Hurrah!' have, or can be given a role in discourse that is primarily descriptive or informative. And if exclamations can on occasion function informatively, normally indicative sentences and predicables may be used, analogously, to "express." It is even more apparent that these functions are not exclusive, and a single utterance may often both describe and express.

Two points should emerge from what has been said thus far: (1) that exclamations may function in certain contexts to convey information or describe a state of affairs; and that the exclamation may replace or be replaced by a syntactically indicative expression without significant alteration in the descriptive force of the utterance; and (2) the test of truth-functional equivalence can be successfully applied—i.e. wherever an exclamation can be substituted for an indicative utterance without significant alteration in descriptive force or informative content, the truth value of the two will be identical.

It seemed essential to ask at the outset what sort of distinction Carnap sought by contrasting representation with expression.[4] And so far I have attempted to establish that, however the lines are drawn, the contrast is meaningful only in an analysis of functions; 'expressive' and 'descriptive,' like 'performative' and 'prescriptive,' qualify linguistic acts and not linguistic components.

It will be the purpose of this chapter to consider the expressive function of language in relation to nonlinguistic expressions and to related but distinguishable linguistic acts.

2 | LET US CONSIDER first the linguistic expression of belief. It will be possible in this way to illustrate how linguistic expressions (expressions in language) differ from related linguistic acts, such as assertions, and from nonverbal behavioral expressions.

Now it follows from the conclusion of the previous chapter that if A expresses the belief that p, he must necessarily have that belief.[5] Assuming that 'A is expressing the

---

[4] I have replaced 'representation' with 'description' in Carnap's scheme. Terminology varies with the authors who have concerned themselves with the problem, but the crucial differences and misunderstandings have not arisen from this terminological preference itself.

[5] Paul Edwards argues that there is an acceptable interpretation of 'expression' which implies that " 'my first class tomorrow starts at ten' would express my belief that my first class starts at ten even if I had no such belief" (*The Logic of Moral Discourse* [New York: The Free Press, 1955], pp. 22-23). I cannot see what sense

belief that p' is true, we are entitled to an inference concerning A: that he is, for example, in a certain psychological state or that he is disposed to act or respond in certain ways, depending on our choice of analysis of the concept of belief. However, since the mere utterance of a proposition does not logically entail the assertion of the proposition, it does not in itself legitimize an inference about the beliefs of the speaker. Geach has maintained that propositions may be present in discourse without being stated assertorically, and yet have the same "content" as the same proposition asserted.[6] 'Assertion' in Geach's argument functions somewhat like 'expression' in the present account, and a syntactically indicative utterance may be no more an assertion than it need be an expression of belief. Simple inspection is never sufficient to guarantee identification of an utterance as either an assertion or an expression. To claim that an assertion (or an expression) has occurred is to claim something more than that certain words have been uttered; it is in fact to claim that a particular kind of inference is warranted.

Assertion and expression are thus closely linked, and it might appear that every instance of the linguistic expression of a belief must also be an assertion of that belief. 'The Hittites were morally inferior to the Maccabees,' ut-

---

can be given to this, or what purpose such an interpretation would serve. It would seem to be, prima facie, meaningless to say that I am expressing *my* belief when there is admittedly no such belief that can be attributed to me.

[6] P. T. Geach, "Assertion," *Philosophical Review*, LXXIV (1965), 449-65. Also see Gottlob Frege, "Compound Thoughts," *Mind*, LXXII (1963), 1-17.

tered assertorically, would also be an expression of the belief that the Hittites were morally inferior to the Maccabees. But this symmetry breaks down in cases where it is possible to express a belief without directly asserting it. 'There will be no ball game today' may, among other things, express my belief that it will rain today, but it does not say so. Or if I should say, 'The whole concert tonight will certainly be boring,' and if it happens that I am bored only by Mozart, then the statement may be an expression of my belief that the program for tonight's concert will consist entirely of works by Mozart. This potential for indirection should help to distinguish expressions of belief from assertions, professions, and affirmations, none of which can be accomplished through a similar kind of indirection.

To talk of the expression of belief then is to authorize an inference about the one who expresses that belief, and the nature of the inference will depend on whatever significance is assigned to the word 'belief.' A dispositional analysis of belief will issue in a set of inferences concerning tendencies or dispositions to act or react in certain ways. A more traditional analysis of belief will result in inferences relating the expression to a certain class of neurological events or psychological states. And others (Austin, perhaps[7]) might urge us to see the *direct* linguistic expression of belief, 'I believe that p,' as a performative act, the giving of a qualified assurance of the truth of a proposition, as opposed to the giving of an unqualified assurance of its truth expressed by 'I know that p.' These

[7] See "Other Minds" and "Truth" in *Philosophical Papers*.

analyses are not logically incompatible, and it is possible that a single occurrence of the expression of belief would entitle us to inferences of all these types.[8]

Now, to bring out more clearly some of the distinguishing features of the linguistic expression of belief I want to explore the dissimilarity of the conditions for the application of the terms 'belief' and 'opinion.' A look at these dissimilarities will reveal the importance of distinguishing between linguistic and nonlinguistic expressions.

Whether we are said to be expressing an opinion or expressing a belief seems often to be of little importance. Perhaps opinions *are* beliefs of a kind. Like beliefs, they advance a weaker claim than knowledge, though we are often prepared to give reasons for them. Thus I may indif-

[8] It may not be clear what sort of inference would be legitimized by a "performative" analysis of belief. If *A* expresses his belief that *p*, and if I take this to be a qualified assurance of its truth, then I may conclude that I cannot hold *A* fully responsible for the consequences, should I act on *p* and discover its falsity. And if *A* himself were committed to a performative analysis of belief expressions, I might infer that he does not wish to grant me the right to hold him responsible. There are probably other inferential possibilities here also. Still I must admit a difficulty with this. If there were any expressions of belief that were purely and only performative, then we would not be entitled to an inference about the speaker himself. There would be nothing "behind" the expression to infer, only the public performance of giving a qualified assurance of the truth of some proposition (as when someone makes a promise, we do not thereby learn something about *him* that we were ignorant of before). But I cannot see any reason to believe that there are, or could be, any expressions of belief which are *merely* performances in this sense. (We *express* beliefs, but we *give*, or *make* promises.) We shall consider later the possibility that there may be other expressions (expressions of something other than belief) which *are* purely performative.

ferently express my belief, or my opinion, that inflation is imminent. And when our kitten looks excitedly toward the door and cries out at the sound of footsteps, I may be tempted to say that he believes his mistress is coming. I might even say that he expresses that belief by the way he behaves. But is there anything here that would tempt us to say he was expressing an *opinion*? And if there is not, does this reveal something extraordinary about opinion?

The talent lacking in my cat—or an infant, or Crusoe's savage—is language. All are capable of possessing and expressing beliefs, but none can possess or express opinions. Is opinion then merely belief which is formulated or formulable in language? And does this imply that there are beliefs resistant to articulation in language? If not, is it senseless then to talk of animals or infants expressing their beliefs? Surely it would be arbitrary to deny without argument that infants and animals have beliefs. Perhaps we should concede that some beliefs at least belong to the behaviorist. Would we be free then to say there are expressions of belief where the belief is not formulated or formulable in language?

It is always conceivable that I, or someone else, would be able to *say* what it is, for example, that my cat believes —he believes that his mistress is at the door; but his expression of that belief does not imply that *he* can formulate that belief in language. If it is true that he believes that his mistress is at the door, it is not true that he must also believe the proposition which asserts that his mistress is at the door. It is rather that we see his behavior *as* an expression of that belief.

It would appear then that there are no beliefs which cannot, in principle, be formulated in language, but this does not mean that the belief must be, or even that it can be formulated by the one who expresses it. On the other hand an opinion, though it may be a belief, must be a belief which is consciously entertained and expressible as a proposition to which the believer gives or withholds assent. An opinion unformulated in language is no opinion at all. This would explain why we speak of 'forming an opinion' but not usually of 'forming a belief.' The conscious process of giving articulate form to a belief is an irreducible part of forming an opinion.[9]

We cannot say, however, that every expression of an opinion is also the expression of a belief. Some value judgments, likings and dislikings, are also expressible as "opinions." (Compare: 'What is your opinion of the Bartok quartets?'; and 'What is your belief about the Bartok quartets?') But here as well, when we speak of a value judgment, preference, or liking as an opinion, we imply that it is expressed or expressible in language and not merely, say, a tendency or disposition. I may express my preference for Bartok over Stravinsky by frequently listening to Bartok and seldom to Stravinsky, but this is not the same as having an opinion of them. Language then is a requisite condition for the possession of opinions, but not for the possession of beliefs.

[9] Opinions are invariantly intentional, i.e. there are no opinions which are not opinions *about* something. Consequently, expressions of opinion (despite the addition of language as a necessary condition) satisfy the criteria developed in Chs. I and II.

It is this lack of equivalence between belief and opinion that Stuart Hampshire overlooks when he writes:

The possibility of having beliefs depends upon the possibility of expressing them in statements. This dependence is not a mere contingent matter of fact, a causal dependence in the common order of nature. It is intrinsic to the concept of belief. No sense could be given to a question about the *beliefs* of beings who possess no language in which to express them, not merely because we could not ascertain their beliefs, but rather because we would not know what would be meant by attributing any specific *opinions* to them. A belief is essentially something that the believer is ready to express in a statement [italics added].[10]

Part of the confusion here results from the indiscriminate alternation of 'belief' and 'opinion.' Hampshire concludes that no meaning could be given to a question about the beliefs of beings unendowed with language "because we would not know what could be meant by attributing any specific *opinions* to them." If we are justified in distinguishing between belief and opinion as I have argued, then Hampshire's contention is misleading and equivocal. Even where it is senseless to attribute a specific opinion to a creature that lacks the means to formulate statements, it may not be similarly pointless to credit him with beliefs. And again, if we are told that beliefs must be formulated in language, we can only protest that it seems clearly possible that some beliefs should be expressed nonlinguistically, in appropriate behavior, and that the requirement that belief be formulable in language can be met without

[10] Stuart Hampshire, *Thought and Action* (New York: Viking, 1960), pp. 141-42.

stipulating that "a belief is essentially something that the *believer* is ready to express in a statement." We can agree that beliefs are always susceptible of formulation in statements without agreeing that the formulation must invariably be enacted by the one who expresses that belief.

Hampshire also argues that the relation between belief and its expression in words is "not a mere contingent matter of fact, . . . The expression of a belief is not the inessential act of clothing it with words; it is the only way of making the belief definite, as a belief in this statement rather than that."[11] If this is taken to mean that the expression of a belief is noncontingent in the sense of being a logically necessary consequence of belief, it is clearly wrong. An unexpressed belief is not a logical absurdity. (Conversely, I have argued that the expression of a nonexistent belief *is* an absurdity.) Also, if a belief which is expressed in words is "a belief in this statement rather than that," we should have to conclude that a belief expressed in words is always equivalent to an *assertion* of "this statement rather than that," and that any statement that expressed a belief would necessarily *assert* that belief as well. But again we have seen how language may express beliefs indirectly yet not imprecisely. Expression and assertion may coincide but they are not interchangeable concepts as Hampshire's argument would seem to imply.

It is important for the study of expression that we insist upon such distinctions as that between belief and opinion. To be a language user is to have the ability to perform a set of actions, among which are expressions of

[11] *Ibid.*, pp. 141, 144.

states of oneself for which there are no analogous behavioral expressions. An expression of the opinion that Morphy could have beaten Fisher (whom he never played) is the expression of a state of the speaker for which there are no uniquely appropriate behavioral expressions.[12] We may contrast this, for example, with the belief that it is about to rain, which is equally expressible in linguistic utterances or by raising an umbrella.[13] Nor are these asymmetries limited to counter-factual beliefs or to beliefs concerning temporally remote occurrences. F. H. Bradley held that relational properties are metaphysically deficient, but it is difficult to see how this belief could have been expressed in Bradley's nonverbal behavior, or how it could have been inferred that he held such a belief in the absence of its linguistic expression.

A belief that is expressible in language alone is also an opinion, and the capacity to have opinions (which is identical with the ability to express them) is evidence of the greater wealth of states that are attributable to language users than to creatures whose expressive capacities are limited to nonverbal behavioral displays.[14]

The ability to express an opinion in language then is a

[12] This point is independent of the analysis of such states.
[13] It should be recalled that to say that behavior expresses a belief, in the way I am using this concept, is to say that the belief and the behavior can be linked inferentially.
[14] This of course is not to say that language is the ideal medium for expressions of all sorts. There are intentional states that are only adequately or fully expressed in nonverbal behavior—sexual desire and hatred, for example. When the behavioral expressions of such states are inhibited or blocked, language may serve as a substitute expression.

necessary condition for having the opinion. But this is not to imply that an opinion must always *be* expressed in language; there may be nonlinguistic expressions of opinion as well. But we consider a person's nonlinguistic behavior an expression of his opinion only if we believe that he *could*, if so inclined, express that opinion in language.

Opinion then represents a class of intentional states that are attributable to language users alone; but it does not exhaust that class. Wishing, regretting, and hoping are equally predicable only of language users. (Compare Wittgenstein's remark: "One can imagine an animal angry, frightened, unhappy, happy, startled. But hopeful? And why not?" "Can only those hope who can talk? Only those who have mastered the use of a language.")[15] What does it mean to say that *only* someone who has mastered a language can hope? Just this: for it to be true that A hopes that p, A must be able to use and understand the expression (or its equivalent) 'I hope that p.' The paradigmatic *expression* of hope is an utterance of the form 'I hope that p'; and in the absence of A's ability to utter or understand such expressions, no sense could be given to 'A hopes that p.' Moreover language, unlike behavior, may allude to the general, the absent, and the nonexistent; and when I wish I had a griffin, or hope that next year will be less tedious, I *do* something for which there are no clear and adequate behavioral expressions;[16] and thus I do something which

---

[15] *Philosophical Investigations*, p. 174e.

[16] Cf. Jonathan Bennett: ". . . *only linguistic behavior can be appropriate or inappropriate to that which is not both particular and present*. . . . The special power of language in these matters derives from the fact that linguistic behavior is behavior which obeys

could not be described as hoping or wishing if I were unable to express my hope or my wish in appropriate linguistic form.

It is characteristic of hoping that we hope only for those outcomes or events which we cannot, or believe we cannot, bring about or ensure through our efforts alone. To hope that p, is among other things to believe that there is some condition for the occurrence of p that I cannot control. If I hope that I will pass my driving test or win the Prix de Rome, then I do not believe that my actions, however efficient, are adequate to ensure my success. Hoping that p differs from *intending* that p just insofar as I believe that there are conditions requisite to the occurrence of p that are somehow beyond my control. My nonlinguistic behavior may express my *intent* to do what I can to secure my license or win the prize, but there is an additional dimension to hoping for these things that cannot be adequately expressed in my nonlinguistic behavior alone. There is nothing I can *do* to express the residual difference between intending to bring about a state of affairs and hoping for its occurrence without employing a linguistic expression, viz. 'I hope that p.'

To hope that p, then, is to be able to say—or inscribe

---

rules correlating performances with empirical states of affairs: and any kind of state of affairs—past or present or future, general or particular—can enter into such a correlation. Non-linguistic behaviour, on the other hand, is necessarily related to states of affairs only in so far as it consists in an attempt to do something about that state of affairs which constitutes the present and particular environment of the behaver" (*Rationality* [New York: Humanities Press, 1964], pp. 87-88).

sincerely a sentence of the form—'I hope that *p*.' And to *be* in a state of "hoping" is, minimally, to be able to use and understand such expressions. It is possible for someone to be hopeful (or wishful or regretful) of something without giving it expression, but it is not possible that he should also lack the *ability* to express it. And the requisite expressive potential lies in the possession of a natural language containing some equivalent of 'I hope . . . ,' 'I wish . . . ,' and 'I regret . . . .' There is obviously more to this than the ability to express such states in language, but I am concerned here only to show how the range of intentional states that are predicable of persons is extended through the acquisition of a language.

3 | To SHARPEN our view of the distinctive features of linguistic expression it will be useful at this point to explore in greater detail the territory where this use of language shades into the neighboring semantic terrain, and in particular, to trace the successive gradations from the expressive through the parenthetical to the performative use of language. Uncovering the contrasts and affinities among these linguistic functions will better enable us to grasp the differentia of linguistic expression.

If I assert that tonight's concert has been canceled, it is clear that in addition to expressing my belief that the concert has been canceled I may also be expressing my disappointment. (Normally *this* expression would be carried by nonsemantic features of the utterance, such as the tone of my voice or the intonation contour.) Now, something similar though more complex occurs when I say, e.g.

'I admire the way you insulted the hostess.' Here the syntactic structure of the sentence contains both a propositional element and a nonpropositional operator. In uttering the sentence (sincerely) I imply that you did in fact insult the hostess and I express my attitude toward your action. The operator in sentences of this type serves to indicate that the implied proposition is qualified by some attitude or feeling. There is no well-established terminology for what I have in mind here, so for convenience I shall refer to such syntactic but nonpropositional qualifiers as E-operators.[17] Thus, in statements such as 'I regret that I shall be unable to attend the wedding,' 'I regret' may occur as an E-operator, i.e., as a semantically direct expression of a qualifying attitude. But it is important to notice that not every utterance prefaced by the words 'I regret' (or 'I hope' or 'I am pleased') can be interpreted in this way. These phrases may also occur *parenthetically*, as Urmson has observed;[18] and 'I regret' may serve not to express an attitude or feeling at all, but merely to introduce the remainder of the utterance in a certain light, as when a messenger must inform a mother that her son has been killed in battle, and says, not, 'Madam, your son is

[17] Russell has advocated classifying all such sentential elements as propositional attitudes (in *An Enquiry into Meaning and Truth*), but this suggests that differences between 'I know' or 'I believe' and 'I desire' or 'I regret' are negligible; and I do not want to imply, as does Russell, that the objects of E-operators are propositional in every case. I do not think, for example, that 'I admire neurologists' can be reformulated in such a way that the object of my admiration takes a propositional form.

[18] J. O. Urmson, "Parenthetical Verbs," *Mind*, LXI (1952), 480-96.

dead,' but 'Madam, I regret that your son is dead.'[19] 'I re-gret' is used here neither expressively nor hypocritically; it serves rather to indicate that the news to be delivered is of a certain (regrettable) nature. A similar parentheti-cal function can be detected in a number of ceremonial uses of language, as when the dean of a university ad-dresses the successful candidates with, 'I am pleased to in-form you that you have passed the examinations.'[20]

What distinguishes the parenthetical use of these senten-tial elements from their use as E-operators is that in the former case it would be pointless to ask whether the state-ment *as a whole* were true or false. Whether the speaker *has* a certain attitude is not at issue where the phrase is parenthetically intended; his sincerity is not at stake, and the question of truth or falsity arises only over the propo-sitional clause contained within the utterance. Where 'I re-gret' or 'I am pleased' or 'I hope' are intended as E-oper-ators, the question of sincerity is relevant, and the issue of truth or falsity shifts from the contained proposition to the utterance as a whole, i.e. to the question whether the speaker does in fact regret, or is pleased that, or hopes that so-and-so is the case.

A further difference between expressions utilizing E-operators and the parenthetical use of language is evident from the way in which they suffer differing fates in the process of tense transformations. Both E-operative and

[19] *Ibid.*

[20] The verb 'express' is itself used parenthetically in a number of ceremonial utterances, as 'Allow me to express my deepest sym-pathy.' The very formality of such constructions intimates that no genuine expression is (or need be) taking place.

parenthetical utterances are limited to the present tense. The E-operators 'I regret' and 'I am pleased' collapse into reports and predictions respectively when the tense is altered to past or future. 'I regretted' and 'I was pleased' no longer express the speaker's regret (or his pleasure)— they merely report their past occurrence. Similarly, 'I will regret' or 'I will be pleased' are predictions, threats, or promises, but not, again, expressions of an occurrent regret or satisfaction.

Now, interestingly, there is no comparable past or future tense for the parenthetical use of these expressions. The past tense of 'I regret that your son was killed in battle' is 'I *regretted* that your son was killed in battle,' and this implies, as the present tense does not, that the speaker had actually experienced regret. And 'I am pleased that . . .' in its past tense form 'I was pleased that . . .' also implies that the speaker was in fact pleased at the time. The use of past (and future) tenses here carries with it the implication that the corresponding present tense utterance is an expression and not a parenthetical remark.

There is no way to report or predict the occurrence of a parenthetical remark by the simple expedient of tense transformation, since the resultant sentences have the wrong implication. But something of the character of parenthetical utterances is brought out in the fact that we can report (or predict) their occurrences by the use of *oratio obliqua*. If I am to describe what the messenger had done, I cannot say simply, 'He regretted to inform her that her son was dead'; but I can avoid the implication of a prior expression on his part by saying, "He said, 'I regret to inform you that your son is dead' "; or, omitting the parenthetical phrase, 'He told her that her son was, unfortunately, dead.'

Admittedly it is often difficult to decide whether a particular sentential element is intended, or is to be taken as a parenthetical remark or an E-operator (e.g. 'I regret that I cannot attend the wedding'). But decisions of this sort are governed by contextual nuances and need not detain us here.

4 | Now, IF IT IS important to distinguish the expressive and the parenthetical uses of language in utterances of the type we have been discussing, it is even more imperative to avoid confounding expressive and performative uses. This point is crucial, for if the expressive use of language is not clearly distinguished from performative utterances both the attempt to establish intentionality as a necessary condition for expression and the argument that an expression is always inference-warranting are threatened; and these points are central to my thesis.

There are a number of similarities between linguistic expressions and performative utterances, however; and the danger of confusing them or assimilating one to the other is sufficiently great to require our attention.[21]

---

[21] It has been a fashionable move in recent philosophy to reclassify recalcitrant linguistic functions as performatives (see e.g. Max Black, "The Gap Between 'Is' and 'Should,'" *Philosophical Review*, LXXIII (1964), pp. 165-81, in which Black attempts to interpret statements containing 'ought' or 'should' as performatives). It is precisely such a reduction of *expressions* to performatives that I shall be concerned to argue against.

R. M. Hare, in criticizing an early emotivist analysis of ethical language, cautions that:

> It is perfectly unexceptionable, on the colloquial plane, to say that the sentence 'A is good' is used to *express* approval of A. . . . but it is philosophically misleading if we think that the approval which is *expressed* is a peculiar warm feeling inside us [italics added].[22]

Hare remarks that, should the Minister of Local Government express approval of my town plan by having a letter sent saying, "The Minister approves of your plan," I would in no circumstances confirm the letter by having a private detective observe the Minister for signs of emotion. "In this case, to have such a letter sent *is* to approve."[23] What Hare is suggesting is that such an "expression" of approval is in fact a performative use of language. The term 'performative,' as is well known, was introduced by Austin to distinguish a class of utterances of which we should say that they were made to *do* something rather than merely to say something.[24] Common examples of performatives, cited by Austin, include 'I promise,' 'I warn,' 'I apologize,' and 'I bet.'

In all these cases it would be absurd to regard the thing that I say as a report of the performance of the action which is undoubtedly done—the action of betting, or christening, or apologizing. We should say rather that, in saying what I do, I actually perform that action. When I say 'I name this ship the *Queen Elizabeth*' I do not describe the christening cere-

[22] R. M. Hare, *The Language of Morals* (Oxford: Clarendon, 1951), p. 10.
[23] *Ibid.*
[24] "Performative Utterances" in *Philosophical Papers.*

mony, I actually perform the christening; and when I say 'I do' (sc. take this woman to be my lawful wedded wife), I am not reporting on a marriage, I am indulging in it.[25]

Austin intended this distinction as an assault on the "descriptive fallacy," the fallacy of regarding all language as inherently descriptive; and he was especially concerned to discredit the attempt to treat certain utterances (the performatives) as deviant descriptions or external signs of inner happenings.

Now, it is not clear that the distinction between the performative and all other uses of language can be sustained consistently, and Austin himself in his later work expressed some dissatisfaction with his analysis.[26] Nevertheless, several features of the distinction have survived intact. Performative utterances are characteristically neither true nor false (or rather it is often difficult to make sense of the question of their truth or falsity), nor are they descriptive in any straightforward way, though they may contain descriptive elements. Where explicit, they occur as first-person, present-tense utterances, and their being uttered under appropriate conditions is sufficient for the truth of a descriptive statement attributing the corresponding action to the speaker. Thus, if A says 'I promise' or 'I bet' in the appropriate setting,[27] the corresponding description ('A promises' or 'A bets') is fully and automatically warranted. No further behavior of A's or disclosures of his

[25] *Ibid.*, p. 222.

[26] *How to Do Things with Words*, ed. J. O. Urmson (New York: Oxford, 1965).

[27] Conditions of appropriateness are often obvious, but see Austin, *How to Do Things with Words*, and below.

state of mind will falsify the description. Breaking the promise or reneging on the bet may be evidence of an unsavory character, but they are no reason for canceling the description. I propose then to adopt these as minimal conditions for the performative use of language.

In the example cited earlier, Hare has implied that the Minister's "expression" of approval is equivalent to a performative use of language (in this case, *bestowing* approval). If Hare is right, then the report that the Minister approved the plan is to be analyzed as claiming: (*a*) that the Minister expressed his approval of the plan, (*b*) that his doing so was a performative act bestowing approval on the plan, and (*c*) that (*a*) and (*b*) are interchangeable and equivalent descriptions of the Minister's action. But I think we must insist that they are not equivalent, since it may be true that the Minister bestowed approval on the plan, and yet false that he expressed his approval.

This point can be brought out in the following way. It would be inconsistent to say '*A* promised to do *x*, but he really didn't promise'; but it is not obviously inconsistent to say '*A* approved *x*, but he doesn't really approve.' In the second case there may be a shift in reference from what *A* *said* to what he thinks or feels about *x*, thereby avoiding the inconsistency. The inconsistency implicit in the first case is explained by the referential identity of the two occurrences of 'promise,' i.e. what *A* *said*. In Hare's example, if it were discovered that the Minister had strong personal objections to my proposal but was nonetheless forced against his judgment to accept my plans, I would be justified in reporting that the Minister *said* he approves, but I know very well he does not. ". . . to have such a letter sent *is* to approve" is in this case either false or ambiguous.

Hare may have been misled by his example. The Minister's "approval" in writing is sufficient to *sanction* the plan. It functions here as a performative and not (necessarily) as an expression. It would be less misleading to say in this instance that the Minister had *given* or *lent* his approval (which is certain) rather than saying that he expressed it (which is not).

What I am cautioning against here is the identification or confusion of performative and expressive uses of language. Expressions, unlike performatives, carry inferential implications about intentional states of the speaker. Ministers may sanction plans, and hence "approve" them, without being favorably disposed toward them, and thus without expressing approval. 'I approve' can, of course, function performatively, but that is no reason to conclude that expressions of approval and performative acts of bestowing approval are one and the same. What Hare appears to have overlooked is that the linguistic expression 'I approve' is not always or necessarily an expression of approval in language. It is worth noting in this connection that we make or give promises, we do not express them; nor do we express bets, christenings, warnings, threats, or commands. We should be able to preserve some distinction then between linguistic acts which can be described as expressions and those which can be described only as performatives.

If performatives and expressions are not identical,

neither are they incompatible, and a single utterance may function in both ways. This occurs in fact whenever a performative utterance is sincere. A promise, given sincerely, is also the expression of an intention, and a sincere apology is an expression of regret, sorrow, or contrition. The possibility that performatives may occur without such correlated expressions is implicit in the concept of insincerity. To say 'I apologize' *is* to apologize, but it may or may not be an expression of regret. Insincerity can be explained in this, and similar cases, as the occurrence of a performative unaccompanied by the appropriate expression. (This does not mean that there is something which, *in addition* to apologizing, I have failed to do, but that there is something which I have failed to do *in* apologizing.)

There are other cases, however, where the question of sincerity would be irrelevant or misplaced (e.g. 'I command . . .' or 'I sentence . . .'). And where such irrelevance exists we can infer that the question of an associated expression is felt to be inappropriate. Judges do not sentence criminals sincerely or insincerely because the feelings of the judge are held to be irrelevant to the exercise of judicial office. There are no conventional expectations that a judge should always accompany the passing of sentence upon an offender with pity or contempt, and consequently no implications to bind the performance to the expression of a particular attitude, intention or feeling, as in promising or apologizing.

Even where the question of sincerity is relevant there are important philosophical differences. To apologize without contrition is less devious than to promise without intent, and less vulnerable to charges of logical or moral impropriety. The difference, I suspect, lies in the expectations aroused by these performances. Where an apology is offered, it is the ceremony itself which is climactic; there is nothing further to await. An apology is a way of putting an end to things, of easing tensions, of repairing damaged relations. But a promise excites expectations of future behavior—expectations of whatever is sufficient to "keep" the promise. The relation between promising and intending is therefore more intimate than that between apologizing and feeling sorry or contrite, and this intimacy is a function of our expectations. An apology may imply contrition, as a promise implies intention, but we concede the difference when we accept apologies which we know to be devoid of regret. It is enough at times that the situation should be saved, without penetrating too deeply into the feelings that accompany the ceremony. Diplomacy is a great arena for the parading of performatives, and we do not always insist that he who apologizes accompany his performance with an inner gesture. Promises, however, are discredited (though not voided) the moment we have reason to suspect the absence of intent. It is clear from this that we are willing to treat these two cases dissimilarly, and we do so because of the differences in what we believe we are entitled to expect, or—what comes to the same—in what we believe the speaker committed to. The force of the implication between promise and intent is greater than that between apology and contrition; there are degrees, shades, and styles of insincerity.

A further difference between performatives and expres-

sions can be located in the varying ways in which they fail
to come off, or suffer some other form of infelicity. Austin
has given considerable attention to the ways in which performatives fail to function "happily" through failing to
meet one or more of a number of requisite conditions. In
Lecture II of *How to Do Things with Words*, he sketches
six such conditions in the form of rules:[28] (1) There must
exist an accepted conventional procedure having a certain
conventional effect, that procedure to include the uttering
of certain words by certain persons in certain circumstances, and further (2) the particular persons and circumstances in a given case must be appropriate for the
invocation of the particular procedure invoked. (3) The
procedure must be executed by all participants both correctly and (4) completely. (5) Where, as often, the procedure is designed for use by persons having certain
thoughts or feelings, or for the inauguration of certain con-
sequential conduct on the part of any participant, then a
person participating in and so invoking the procedure must
in fact have those thoughts or feelings, and the participants
must intend so to conduct themselves, and further (6)
must actually so conduct themselves subsequently.

Failure to comply with one or more of these rules will
result in some measure of "unhappiness" or infelicity in
the performative utterance. These rules can be further
grouped into two categories—those whose infraction results in failure to accomplish the intended action (failure
of the performative to come off), and those whose infrac-

[28] I have altered the numbering of these rules, though not the
sequence.

tion does not nullify the act but qualifies it as insincere.[29] I will fail to marry even though I utter the words 'I do' in the appropriate circumstances if, say, I am already married (Rules 1-4). But if I thank someone effusively, though without gratitude, I have not failed to thank him; I have only done so insincerely (Rules 5-6).

Now expressions may be "unhappy" through being false, unsuccessful, inappropriate, unapt, exaggerated, or insincere. False expressions are like false friends (and unlike false promises). False smiles are false expressions because they fail to express what they *purport* to express, as in the hostess's smile at the unwelcome guest. A false promise is one that is insincere or deceitful, but a promise nonetheless. Unsuccessful expressions resemble false expressions in failing to express, though here there is an implication of intent to express. I want to express my annoyance but I am too inhibited, so the inclination is dissipated in fidgeting. (Of course one might object that such displaced activity as fidgeting is still expressive of my annoyance, but then we shall still need a place for the notion of an unsuccessful expression as one which fails to realize intentions in appropriate behavior.) Unapt or exaggerated expressions fall under the general condition of inappropriateness. There are vast possibilities, obviously, for inappropriate expressions, but inappropriate, unlike false and unsuccessful expressions are still expressions, though unhappy in other ways. On the other hand, the conditions which

---

[29] This is merely the skeleton of Austin's argument. I have made no attempt to condense the rich texture of examples and distinctions which enliven his book.

render a performative inappropriate usually nullify it as well. A command issued by an officer to a civilian outside his authority is issued inappropriately, and fails to come off (i.e. fails to *be* the intended action). But an inappropriate expression, no matter how bizarre, is still an expression. (Voicing my unrestrained glee over the cakes at the funeral may be grotesque, but it is not void as an expression.)

Differences emerge then in the conditions under which a performative and an expression may succeed or fail. Among the conditions cited by Austin for the happy execution of a performative are the existence of conventional procedures, circumstances and relationships, and the ordered following of prescribed ceremonies. Moreover many performatives depend for their validity upon the possibility of successful communication. I cannot be said to have congratulated you or begged your pardon or given you my word unless you were in a position to hear and understand my utterance.[30] A faulty performative, however, may be a genuine expression: If I 'give you my word' that I will be faithful while you are miles away and unmindful of my promise, I may yet be expressing my intentions, my hopes, or my fears.

Expression is *not* communication; nor does it require communication to occur successfully. I may intend or

---

[30] This is quite different from the *effect* that my words may have on the hearer (Austin's perlocutionary force). The communication requirement is merely that the hearer be in a position to hear my remarks and take them to be a compliment, an insult, or a promise. The effect of my words may be to amuse, annoy, or bore him, but that is another matter.

hope to communicate something by saying (or doing) what I do, but it is not a condition of expression that this should be so, or that I should succeed.

Finally, insincere expressions can be assimilated to false expressions. An apology or a promise, given insincerely, is still an apology or a promise, but the insincere expression of admiration is hollow flattery, and no expression at all.

An awareness of these differences between the expressive and performative functions of linguistic acts should dispel the temptation to collapse one into the other, and enable us to preserve the autonomy of these importantly disparate concepts.

5 | THESE DISTINCTIONS can hardly be said to exhaust the issues that arise over the peculiarities of linguistic expression, but they constitute a conceptual triangulation in which linguistic expressions can be located in relation to other language acts and to nonlinguistic behavioral expressions. Linguistic expression, like its behavioral counterpart, preserves an inferential connection with intentional states of the person, and what they share in common distinguishes the linguistic act of expression from related but logically distinct classes of linguistic acts. Where linguistic and behavioral expressions part company we can discern those particular states of persons for which language provides not an alternate means of expression but the necessary and singular means.

Whatever further questions are raised must, I think, presuppose that we have gotten at least this far.

CHAPTER **IV** ART AND
EXPRESSION:
A CRITIQUE

1 | IF THE ANALYSIS developed in preceding chapters is correct in its general outlines, it should be possible to derive from it a number of implications bearing on the adequacy of attempts to understand art as a form of expression.

The history of the philosophy of art could, without excessive distortion, be written as a study of the significance of a handful of concepts. The successive displacement of 'imitation' by 'representation,' and of 'representation' by 'expression,' for example, marks one of the more revealing developments in the literature of aesthetics; and it would be only a slight exaggeration to claim that from the close of the eighteenth century to the present 'expression' and its cognates have dominated both aesthetic theorizing and the critical appraisal of the arts. One purpose of this chapter will be to explore the claim that works of art or the activities of the artist can best be understood as a form of expression.

2 | LET US FIRST consider some of the contentions of philosophers who have advanced expression theories of art. It has generally been recognized that some distinction must be made at the outset between the process and the product of art: we must distinguish between the artist's activity in constructing a work of art and the outcome of that activity, the work itself. It matters, that is, whether 'expression' is predicated of the process, the product, or both. Many, including Dewey, Reid, Ducasse, Santayana,

and Collingwood,[1] have been explicit about this distinction, and have advocated predicating 'expression' of both process and product. These writers are committed to maintaining that there is a noncontingent and specifiable relation between the artist's activity and the work of art. More precisely, they are committed to the position that the artist, in creating the work, is expressing something,[2] which is then to be found "embodied," "infused," or "objectified" in the work itself. For such theorists, the "central problem of the aesthetic attitude" is "how a feeling can be got into an object"[3] or, alternately, how the artist in expressing his feelings embodies them in the art work.

Common to all theories of this type are two assumptions: (1) that an artist, in creating a work of art, is invariably engaged in expressing something; and (2) that the expressive qualities of the art work are the direct consequence of this act of expression. I shall argue that there is no reason to accept these assumptions; but first we must consider a logically prior contention which is almost universally accepted by Expression theorists. This contention is that aesthetic, or artistic expression is something quite different from the symptomatic behavioral display of inner states.[4] Vincent Tomas summarizes this view in these words:

---

[1] See the bibliography for citations of the relevant works.

[2] There is a range of values for the variable here; 'feeling,' 'attitude,' 'idea,' 'mood,' and 'outlook' have all been suggested at some time, but 'feeling' is the favored substitution.

[3] Bernard Bosanquet, *Three Lectures on Aesthetic* (London: Macmillan, 1915), p. 74.

[4] Cf. Ch. 1 on the distinction between expressions and signs or symptoms.

98

... behavior which is merely symptomatic of a feeling, such as blushing when one is embarrassed or swearing when one is angry, is not artistic expression of feeling. Collingwood says it is just a "betrayal" of feeling. Dewey says it is "just a boiling over" of a feeling, and Ducasse says it is "a merely impulsive blowing off of emotional steam." As Hospers says, "A person may give vent to grief without expressing grief." Unlike merely giving vent to or betraying a feeling, artistic expression consists in the deliberate creation of something which "embodies" or "objectifies" the feeling.[5]

The corollary is that "embodying" or "objectifying" a feeling is equivalent to (artistically) expressing it. It is important to notice that these distinctions have been made in the interest of sustaining some favored version of the Expression theory; and since the appropriation of 'expression' for this purpose involves a significant departure from ordinary usage, we may reasonably demand some justification for this procedure.

On this point Dewey is the most thorough and articulate, and I shall confine my criticism to his version of the argument. Dewey writes that:

Not all outgoing activity is of the nature of expression. At one extreme, there are storms of passion that break through barriers and that sweep away whatever intervenes between a person and something he would destroy. There is activity, but not, from the standpoint of the one acting, expression. An onlooker may say "What a magnificent expression of rage!" But the enraged being is only raging, quite a different matter

[5] "The Concept of Expression in Art," *Philosophy Looks at the Arts*, ed. Joseph Margolis (New York: Scribner's, 1962), p. 31. The quotations are taken from Collingwood, *The Principles of Art*; Dewey, *Art as Experience*; Ducasse, *Art, the Critics, and You*; and Hospers, *Meaning and Truth in the Arts*.

from *expressing* rage. Or, again, some spectator may say "How that man is expressing his own dominant character in what he is doing or saying." But the last thing the man in question is thinking of is to express his character; he is only giving way to a fit of passion.[6]

Dewey is concerned to protect us from the "error" which has invaded aesthetic theory ". . . that the mere giving way to an impulse, native or habitual, constitutes expression."[7] He adds that "emotional discharge is a necessary but not a sufficient condition of expression" on the grounds that: "While there is no expression, unless there is urge from within outwards, the welling up must be clarified and ordered by taking into itself the values of prior experiences before it can be an act of expression."[8] There can be no expression without inner agitation then, but the mere discharging of inner impulses is insufficient to constitute an expression. ". . . to express is to stay by, to carry forward in development, to work out to completion";[9] and, "Where there is . . . no shaping of materials in the interest of embodying excitement, there is no expression."[10]

Dewey offers these remarks as *evidence* for the adequacy of the Expression theory, whereas they follow in fact only if one has already assumed its truth. They are thinly disguised stipulations and not, as Dewey would have it, independently discoverable truths *about* expression. The circularity of this procedure can best be seen in his refusal to admit anything as an expression which does not result in the production of an object or state of affairs that

---

[6] *Art as Experience*, p. 61.
[7] *Loc.cit.*   [8] *Loc.cit.*   [9] *Ibid.*, p. 62.   [10] *Loc.cit.*

embodies some aesthetically valuable quality.[11] But there are more serious objections. Dewey clearly wants to confine 'expression' to activities which are intentionally or voluntarily undertaken. (It must be an expression "from the standpoint of the one acting"; the involuntary venting of rage is ruled out with the comment that "the last thing the man in question is thinking of is to express his character; he is only giving way to a fit of passion.") But there is an existing distinction, and one which we would normally employ here, between voluntary and involuntary expression.[12] Dewey offers us no reason for abandoning this in favor of his stipulative restriction, other than an implicit appeal to the very theory which requires the sacrifice, and we are entitled to a more compelling argument before adopting this way of speaking.[13]

One reason for Dewey's insistence on this restriction is obvious. Many activities and behavioral patterns that are called 'expressions' are irrelevant to the production of aesthetically interesting objects. Most Expression theorists agree that the artist is engaged in doing something quite different from the man who merely vents his rage or airs his opinions—that he is doing something which bears little resemblance to commonly recognized varieties of expressive behavior. But the fact that the artist *is* doing

[11] Chs. IV and V of *Art as Experience*.

[12] See my remarks on this distinction in Ch. II, Section I.

[13] Dewey makes more of this than most Expression theorists, but even those, like Ducasse, who admit the use of 'expression' to describe involuntary revelations of inner states have argued that *aesthetic* expression is something quite distinct, and not to be confused with the former.

101

something so apparently different ought to suggest not that he alone is expressing while others are not, but that the aesthetically relevant activity of the artist may not be an expression at all. Rather than being shown in creative activity the real meaning of 'expression,' we are offered a stipulation which would undermine most of the paradigmatic examples of expressive behavior in the interests of promoting a debatable theory.

The upshot of this is that, if "aesthetic expression" as a process is not to be understood in relation to pre-analytic notions of expressive behavior, then it must be understood in relation to something else—the something else here being the aesthetic qualities of the created product, the work of art.

In turning to the expressive qualities of the object we are not leaving behind the act of expression, for even if we center attention on the properties of the work itself ("the object that is expressive, that says something to us"[14]) Dewey reminds us that "isolation of the act of expressing from the expressiveness possessed by the object leads to the notion that expression is merely a process of discharging personal emotion"[15]; and that, "Expression as personal act and as objective result are *organically connected* with each other [italics added]."[16] But it is just here that Expression theories fail to convince, for the nature of this supposed connection is far from obvious, and no adequate analysis has yet been offered by anyone committed to this view. The argument for such a connection is usually estab-

[14] Dewey, *Art as Experience*, p. 82.
[15] *Loc.cit.*   [16] *Loc.cit.*

102

lished somewhat in the following way: aesthetic objects, including works of art, are said to possess certain perceptible physiognomic or "expressive" qualities such as 'sadness,' 'gaiety,' 'longing'; and where these are qualities of intentionally structured objects it is reasonable to assume that their presence is the intended consequence of the productive activity of the artist. But the Expression theorist is not content with this; he will go on to assert that, since the aesthetically relevant qualities of the object are *expressive* qualities, the productive activity must have been an act of expression and, moreover, an act of expressing just those feeling states whose analogues are predicated of the object. The situation can be represented more schematically in the following way:

> (*E-T*) If art object O has expressive quality Q, then there was a prior activity C of the artist A such that in doing C, A expressed his F for X by imparting Q to O (where F is a feeling state and Q is the qualitative analogue of F).

The *E-T* represents a core-theory which I believe to be shared e.g. by Dewey, Ducasse, Collingwood, Carritt, Gotshalk, Santayana, Tolstoy, and Véron, whatever their further differences might be.[17] I shall argue that the *E-T*

[17] Harold Osborne has summarized the Expression theory in a somewhat different manner: "The underlying theory is, in its baldest form, that the artist lives through a certain experience; he then makes an artifact which in some way embodies that experience; and through appreciative contemplation of this artifact other men are able to duplicate in their own minds the experience of the artist. What is conveyed to them is . . . an experience of their own as similar as possible to the artist's experience in all its as-

contains an error traceable to the tendency to treat all of the cognate forms of 'expression' as terms whose logical behavior is similar. The particular mistake here arises from assuming that the existence of *expressive qualities* in a work of art implies a prior act of *expression*.

Now, to say that an object has a particular expressive quality is to say something, first of all, about the object. (Even those who argue that 'the music is sad' can be translated as 'the music makes me feel sad' or '. . . has a disposition to make me, or others, feel sad' will agree that their accounts are only plausible on the assumption that the object has *some* properties which are at least causally relevant to the induced feeling.) But the Expression theorist is committed to the further assumption of a *necessary* link between the qualities of the art work and certain states of the artist. Critics of this theory have been quick to observe that this would commit us to treating all art works as autobiographical revelations. Moreover, it would entail that descriptions of the expressive qualities of an art work were falsifiable in a peculiar way. If it turned out that Mahler had experienced *no* state of mind remotely resembling despair or resignation during the period of the composition of *Das Lied von der Erde*, the Expression theorist would be obliged to conclude that we were mistaken in saying that the final movement (*Der Abschied*) of that

---

pects . . ." (*Aesthetics and Criticism* [London: Routledge and Kegan Paul, 1955], p. 143). My formulation is constructed to call attention to the Expression theorist's view of the relation between the activity of the artist and the expressive qualities of the work. (See Appendix for a collection of representative passages from the writings of Expression theorists.)

work was expressive of despair or resignation; and this seems hardly plausible, since it implies that statements ostensibly about the music itself are in fact statements about the composer.[18] If works of art *were* expressions, in the way that behavior and language are expressions of states of a person, that is precisely what we would say. Normal imputations of expression *are* falsifiable, and the assertion that a person's behavior constitutes an expression of something is defeated when it can be shown that the imputed inference is unwarranted.[19] But statements about the expressive qualities of an art work remain, irresolutely, statements *about* the work, and any revision or rejection of such statements can be supported only by referring to the work itself. 'That's a sad piece of music' is countered not by objections such as, 'No, he wasn't' or 'He was just pretending' (referring to the composer), but by remarking 'You haven't listened carefully' or 'You must listen again; there are almost no minor progressions and the tempo is *allegro moderato.*'

Descriptions attributing expressive qualities to works of art then are not subject to falsification through the discovery of any truths about the inner life of the artist. An Expression theorist could of course grasp the other horn, arguing that the presence of quality Q in O is *sufficient*

---

[18] If it is objected that the composer is expressing some *remembered* or unconscious feelings of this sort, we can strengthen the example by supposing it to be false that the composer had ever experienced, consciously or otherwise, the feeling corresponding to the feeling-quality attributed to the music. The logical point remains untouched in any case.

[19] See Ch. ii.

evidence of the occurrence of state S in A, such that A felt F for X. But in ruling out the possibility of independent and conflicting evidence of the artist's feeling states, the Expression theorist secures his position by the simple expedient of making it analytically true; and no one, to my knowledge, has wished to claim that the $E\text{-}T$ is an empty, though indisputable truth.

That a theory of art-as-expression which entails these difficulties should have been embraced so widely is due in part to a misunderstanding of the logic of 'expression' and 'expressive.' I would argue that statements attributing expressive (or physiognomic) properties to works of art should be construed as statements about the works themselves;[20] and that the presence of expressive properties does not entail the occurrence of a prior *act* of expression. Misunderstanding of this latter point has contributed greatly to the uncritical acceptance of the $E\text{-}T$.

3 | 'EXPRESSIVE,' despite its grammatical relation to 'expression,' does not always play the logical role that one might expect. There are occasions on which the substitution of one term for the other is semantically harmless. 'His gesture was an expression of impatience' may in some contexts be replaced without noticeable alteration in meaning by 'His gesture was expressive of impatience.' But there are other contexts in which 'expression' and 'expressive' are significantly disparate. The remark that 'Livia has a very expressive face' does not entail that Livia is especially adept at expressing her inner states, nor does

[20] Albeit rather complex statements, as we shall see in Ch. v.

it entail that she is blessed with an unusually large reper-
toire of moods and feelings which she displays in a continuous kaleidoscope of facial configurations.

To make this clear I shall need to appeal to another distinction, developed in an earlier chapter,[21] between the
two syntactic forms, 'ϕ expression' (A) and 'expression
of ϕ' (B). That distinction was intended to establish that
instances of B are inference-warranting while instances of
A are descriptive, and that A and B are logically independent in the sense that no statement containing an instance of A (or B) entails another statement containing
an instance of B (or A). (A cruel expression in a human
face does not automatically entitle us to infer that cruelty
is being expressed.)

Now, the assertion that a person has an expressive face
is not equivalent to the assertion that he is expressing, or
is disposed to express, his inner states through a set of
facial configurations; or rather the equivalence is not guar-
anteed. The difficulty is that 'expressive' is systematically
ambiguous. It *may* be an alternate reading of 'is an expression of . . .' or it may be understood as a one-place predicate with no inferential overtones. Which of these meanings it has in a particular instance will depend upon what
substitutions we are willing to make and what further
questions we are prepared to admit. If, for example, the
question 'expressive of what?' is blocked, we can conclude
that 'expressive' is not functioning here in a variant of
syntactic form B. 'X is expressive' does not *entail* that
there is an inner state S such that S is being expressed, any

---

[21] Cf. Ch. ii.

more than the appearance of a cruel expression in a face entails that cruelty is being expressed.

The statement that 'X is express*ive*' then may be logically complete, and to say of a person's gesture or face that it is *expressive* is not invariably to legitimize the question 'expressive of what?' In such cases we may say that 'expressive' is used intransitively. Still, we would not call a face (intransitively) expressive unless it displayed considerable mobility. A face that perpetually wore the *same* expression would not be expressive, and appreciation of this point should contribute to an understanding of the intransitive (*I*) sense of 'expressive.' A face is expressive (*I*) when it displays a wide range of expressions (*A*). Thus the successive appearance of sad, peevish, sneering, and puzzled expressions on the face of a child may lead us to say that he has an expressive face without committing us to a set of implications about the inner state of the child.

The meaning of 'expressive' (*I*) is not exhausted, however, through correlation with indefinitely extended sets of expressions (*A*). A face may be expressive merely in virtue of its mobility or its range of perceptible configurations, even though it presents no recognizable expressions (*A*) for which there are established names. To this extent, 'expressive' (*I*) is dispositional. It refers to the disposition of a face (or a body) to assume a variety of plastic configurations regardless of whether any momentary aspect of the face is describable as an expression (*A*) or not; and since it is clear that we have neither names nor definite descriptions for many of the geometrical patterns the human face and body can assume, the domain of 'expressive' (*I*) is both wider and less precise than 'expression' (*A*). It may refer at times simply to the capacity or disposition of a person to move or use his body in varied and perceptually interesting ways.[22] But whatever the correct analysis of 'expressive' (*I*), the fact remains that its use imposes no inferential commitments, and we may use it, just as we use 'expression' (*A*) to refer to certain qualities of persons and objects without implying the existence of some correlated *act* of expression.

4 | IT MAY BE objected that all this, at best, discloses some interesting features of the use of 'expression' and 'expressive' in ordinary language which, from the standpoint of the Expression theorist, are entirely irrelevant. On the contrary, I believe these distinctions are crucial for an understanding of the very art form to which Expression theorists have made most frequent appeal. The point I want to develop here is that the language used by composers and performers of music is at variance with the conception of musical activity derivable from the *E-T*. This is not merely an instance of the naïveté of artists in contrast with the ability of philosophers to provide reflective analyses of a complex enterprise. It is rather that 'expressive' has a particular and quasi-technical meaning *within* the language used by musicians—a meaning which is logically similar to the intransitive sense of 'expressive,'

[22] Notice e.g. that we can refer to the movements of a Thai dancer performing a *Lakon* as expressive even though we may have no idea what the movements "mean" and no precise language in which to describe them.

which is clearly distinguishable from 'expression' (*B*), and whose use does not therefore commit us to any version of the *E-T*.

There are numerous passages in the music of the Romantic period (and later) which are marked *espressivo* ("expressively" or "with expression"). Now this is a particular instruction for the performance of the indicated passage or phrase, and as such it can be compared with the instructions *agitato, grazioso, dolce, leggiero, secco, stürmisch, schwer*, and *pesante*. All of these are indications to the performer that the passage is to be played in a certain manner, and to play *espressivo* is merely to play in one manner rather than another. It is not to play well rather than badly, or to play with, rather than without some particular feeling, nor is it to succeed rather than fail to communicate the composer's intentions, feelings, or ideas. All of these misconceptions are the result of a category mistake. One does not play *agitato* or *pesante and espressivo*; the choice must come from among alternatives all of which are logically similar members of a single category.[23] Moreover, to play *espressivo* is not to be engaged in expressing anything, any more than to play *leggiero* is

[23] Many of the commonly encountered instructions for performance are incompatible, though of course this is not true of all. *Leggiero* and *animoso* are clearly compatible, and the opening bars of Debussy's *Prélude à 'L'Après-Midi D'Un Faune'* are marked *doux et expressif*; but the indication '*secco, espressivo*' would be contradictory, and contradictory in the same way that incompatible imperatives are contradictory—the performer could not simultaneously carry out both instructions.

to express lightness. (Nor, similarly does the composition of an expressive work entail that the *composer* be expressing anything.) Failure to realize this has led some adherents of the Expression theory into associating an expressive musical performance with some presumed *act* of expression on the part of the performer, the composer, or both, and thence with some particular feeling state which is attributable to them.[24]

It would follow from the *E-T* that we might always be mistaken in thinking that a performer had played a phrase expressively, since the correctness of this belief would depend on the truth of some psychological statement about the performer's inner states. But *espressivo* (expressively) is an adverbial characterization of a *manner* of performance, and the suggestion that follows from the *E-T*, that an expressive performance *must* be linked noncontingently to some particular inner state of the performer, is untenable.

It might be objected at this point that both the Expression theorist and I have misconceived the role of 'expressive,' for in critical usage 'expressive' may characterize entire performances or personal styles of performance (one might argue that Oistrakh's performance of the Sibelius *Violin Concerto* was more expressive than Heifetz's, or that generally, *A*'s playing was more expressive than *B*'s). 'Expressive' is still intransitive in this role, but it resists

---

[24] When the difficulty of naming particular feeling states becomes apparent, the Expression theorist may resort to the sui generis category of "aesthetic emotions."

reduction to specific occurrences of passages played *espressivo*.[25] And it is this usage which may lead to the suggestion that 'expressive' has a primarily *evaluative* function in critical discourse. 'Expressive' does not, on this view, license inferences nor label particular or even general features of the object to be assessed, rather it does the assessing. Thus, calling a performance expressive would be to approve, applaud, or commend, not to detect, notice, or describe.

But there are two related and, I think, decisive objections to this suggestion. For even where 'expressive' is used to characterize a style or an entire performance and cannot be explicated by reference to particular occurrences of *espressivo* passages, the possibility remains that the expressiveness may be misplaced. There are omnipresent opportunities for misplaced expressiveness in musical performances, and we should find something peculiarly offensive in an expressive performance of Stravinsky's *L'Histoire du Soldat* or Bartok's *Allegro Barbaro*. Appropriate and effective performances of such works require the absence, or perhaps even the deliberate suppression of expressiveness. Similarly, austere performances of austere works are not *bad* performances; and to call performances of such works expressive may well be to condemn them. If 'expressive' were primarily an evaluative device, the notion of misplaced expressiveness would be self-contradictory, or at best paradoxical. Similar remarks apply to works as well as performances, and describing a particu-

---

[25] There is a strong analogy between the intransitively expressive performance and the intransitively expressive face.

lar work as nonexpressive is not equivalent to condemning it, nor is it prima facie evidence of its lack of artistic worth.

The second error results from failure to notice the first. Whether 'expressive' may be correctly *used* to praise a performance is a function of whether an expressive performance is appropriate to the work being performed. Where it *is* appropriate, and the performance commensurately expressive, *calling* it so may also serve to commend it. But this does no more to show that 'expressive' is an essentially evaluative predicate of our critical language than commending figs for their sweetness shows that 'sweet' is an essentially evaluative predicate of our culinary language. That we prefer expressive to nonexpressive performances of Rachmaninoff and Chopin implies that we regard expressiveness as required for an appropriate reading of the Romantic architecture of their works; it does not imply that 'expressive' is an aesthetic variant of 'good.'

We shall gain a better view of the issue, I think, if we consider how we might teach someone to play expressively or, conversely, how we might teach someone to recognize an expressive performance. If a student asks: 'What must I do to play this passage expressively?' we cannot give him a rule to follow such as: 'You must always play such passages in *this* way . . .' Of course we can give him a rule of sorts—'To play expressively you must vary the dynamics of the phrase; you must stress some notes more than others, and you must not play with rhythmic rigidity'— but we cannot give him a precise rule specifying *which* notes to stress or where and how to vary the dynamics.

There are no paradigmatic examples of expressive playing from which a universal rule could be extracted and applied to other phrases. No phrase can be played expressively without *some* deviation from literal note values, without *some* modulations in the dynamic level, but the choice of where and how is not rule-governed.[26] The student who merely follows our second-order rule and plays the passage with rhythmic freedom and some dynamic modulation may produce a grotesquely unmusical and inexpressive result.

The problem is analogous to teaching someone to recognize an expressively played passage. There are no rules that will help here either. (If someone had no idea what to listen for, we might say: 'It happens when the pianist closes his eyes' or 'Watch for him to sway from the waist' and so on.) It may be thought that the difficulty here is much the same as that of showing the face in the cloud to someone whose aspect-blindness allows him to perceive only the cloud. There is an analogous kind of expression-deafness, but the analogy is only partial, and it is apt to mislead. Expression-deafness is closer to aspect-blindness than to color-blindness. There is no way to *teach* a color-blind person to see the normal range of colors, but we may succeed in getting someone to see the face in the cloud or the 'aspects' of the duck-rabbit figure; and we may succeed, analogously, in teaching someone to recognize

[26] See Frank Sibley, "Aesthetic Concepts," *Philosophical Review*, LXVIII (1959), 421-50, for a cogent discussion of the general question of rule-governed and sufficient conditions in aesthetic discourse.

an expressive performance. But the analogy cannot be stretched to a perfect fit. Recognition of the expressiveness in Grumiaux's performance of the Debussy *Sonata for Violin and Piano* presupposes that we are able to discriminate among a number of qualities that are predicable of musical performances. To hear a performance as expressive is also to hear that it is *not* dry, strained, heavy, agitated, or hollow. The identification presupposes, in other words, that we are conversant with a highly complex set of predicates and with their logical relations to one another. Recognition of the duck in the duck-rabbit figure, on the other hand, seems not to presuppose any comparably complex discriminatory abilities. Ducks and duck-like shapes may be recognizable even to those whose acquaintance with the zoological world is limited to ducks. But talk of expressive performances or works can occur meaningfully only within a developed language of musical criticism, and it implies an ability to discriminate and select from among a number of logically similar predicates.

There is no possibility that someone should learn to use 'expressive' correctly and yet be unable correctly to apply any other aesthetic predicate, as one might learn to use 'duck' correctly without at the same time being able to correctly apply other zoological predicates. (Seeing the figure as a duck is more closely analogous to hearing the sounds as music than to hearing the music as expressive.)

Aesthetic predicates are not learned independently of one another in some discursive or ostensive fashion. They acquire significance for us only in relation to one another

115

as we become reflective and articulate participants in the art world.[27]

Despite the popularity of aspect and "seeing-as" models in recent discussions of aesthetic perception, considerations such as this seriously impair the attempt to explain our perception of aesthetic qualities by analogy with the perception of aspects, or as instances of "seeing-as."[28] Aspect perception has been a useful model in freeing us from the temptation to think of aesthetic objects as ontologically peculiar and distinct from, say, the material objects we hang on our walls; but it is misleading when it suggests that seeing, or hearing, an art work as *expressive* (or garish, or sentimental) is no different from spotting the face in the cloud or the duck in the figure.

5 | THE EXPRESSION theorist of course may object that he is not concerned so much with the language of musicians or critics as with the possibility of giving a theoretical description of the art which would enable us to grasp certain aesthetically relevant features of the processes of creating, performing, and attending to musical compositions. We must, I think, admit that there is a sense

[27] See also Arthur C. Danto, "The Artworld," *Journal of Philosophy*, LXI (1964), 571-84.

[28] See e.g. B. R. Tilghman, "Aesthetic Perception and the Problem of the 'Aesthetic Object,'" *Mind*, LXXV (1966), 351-68; and Virgil C. Aldrich, *Philosophy of Art* (Englewood Cliffs: Prentice-Hall, 1963). A recent illustration of some of the limitations of aspect-perception models in aesthetics may be found in Peter Kivy, "Aesthetic Aspects and Aesthetic Qualities," *Journal of Philosophy*, LXV (1968), 85-93. The *locus classicus* for discussions of the problem is Wittgenstein, *Philosophical Investigations*, Part II.

in which it would be correct to say that a piece of music may be an expression (B); the account I have given in the preceding chapters leaves open this possibility. But this admission concedes nothing to the *E-T*, for the only sense in which 'expression' (B) is admissible here is inconsistent with the *E-T*.

The admission amounts to this: Aside from certain occurrences of nonverbal behavior and linguistic utterances there is a class of things we may call indirect or secondary expressions. The manner of a woman's dress, the way she wears her hair, or the arrangement of her room may "express" some aspect of her character. My handwriting, my preferences in literature, my style at poker, and my choice of friends may likewise reveal something of my inner states and dispositions. It is legitimate to speak of these as expressions (B) where they satisfy the conditions of being evidential or inference-warranting, and lead, correctly, to the attribution of an intentional state.[29] It is clear that this is often the case, that we do make such inferences, and that the conditions for expression are satisfied here as well as in cases of direct or primary expression in language and behavior.

And if my style of playing poker expresses my temerity or my avarice, why should not my style of painting landscapes express something of me as well? Or my style of playing the flute? The conditions of a warranted inference to an intentional state may be as well met by art as by action; and there are impressive examples in the literature of psychoanalysis of the use of art works to unlock the

[29] Cf. Chs. I and II.

psychic labyrinths of the artist.[30] It is this sense in which I concede that an art work may be an expression of something: it may contribute material leading to a correct inference to an intentional state of the artist. But I contend that this does nothing to support the *E-T*, and further, that it does nothing to distinguish art from any other product of human activity.

We should recall that the *E-T* entails that the (successful) artist, by his creative activity, imparts a quality to the work which is *descriptively analogous* to the feeling state expressed by him (sadness-'sadness') and ought therefore to be recognizable as the embodiment of his feeling without assistance from extra-perceptual sources of knowledge. But, far from being clear that this is always the case with successful works of art, it would seem in some instances to be impossible. It will be best to illustrate this point with an example. Carl Nielsen completed his Sixth Symphony during the years 1924-25, and it was during this period of the composer's life that "he was harassed by ill health and depression, puzzled by the notoriety enjoyed by what seemed to him to be musical nihilism, and upset over the seeming failure of his own work to take hold beyond the borders of his native land. . . . It is not unreasonable to suppose that this is the source of some of the exasperation that manifests itself particularly in the second and

[30] Freud's study of Leonardo is perhaps the best known of such attempts; but Jung has made more consistent use of art works in his routine analytic practice. Cf. particularly *Symbols of Transformation*, tr. R.F.C. Hull, Bollingen Series xx:5 (New York: Pantheon, 1956).

final movements of the Sixth Symphony."[31] (The second movement is referred to later as ". . . a bitter commentary on the musical modernism of the 1920's.")

Now the second movement of the Nielsen symphony is marked *Humoresque,* and the prevailing impression left by the music itself is that of lighthearted buffoonery. It may not be unreasonable as the program notes suggest, to conclude that Nielsen was venting exasperation, bitterness, or disappointment here, but it is difficult to see how such an inference could have been suggested by attending to the qualities of the music alone. The music does not *sound* exasperated or disappointed, nor can I see how any piece of music *could* have these as perceptible qualities. The movement sounds humorous, and there is an obvious reference to Prokofiev's *Peter and the Wolf;* but the suggestion that Nielsen was manifesting exasperation or commenting bitterly on musical modernism in this piece can have arisen only with the acquisition of some extramusical information about the composer's life. If the critic *now* wants to maintain that the Sixth Symphony is an expression of Nielsen's bitterness and disappointment, we may agree that this is at least a plausible inference given the truth of the biographical data. But we must also point out that this has little to do with the aesthetically relevant expressive qualities of the music itself. This is something of a paradox for the *E-T.* In order for the Nielsen sym-

---

[31] Quoted from the notes to *Music of the North,* Vol. viii: Carl Nielsen, Symphony No. 6, "Sinfonia Semplice," Mercury Classics Recording, MG 10137.

phony to be an expression of the composer's bitterness and disappointment (i.e., to be a secondary expression) it must have certain perceptible qualities which, together with the biographical data, will yield an inference. But the qualities of the music here are not, and *cannot* be analogues of the intentional state of the composer. The music is humorous, the composer is disappointed. And he cannot inject his bitterness and disappointment into the music in the way that is required by the *E-T*. There is no sense in which the *music* is disappointed. Even if we suppose it to be true that Nielsen was disappointed, exasperated, or bitter, and that the critic's inferences are correct, there is nothing in this to establish the presence of a noncontingent relation between the perceptible qualities of the music and any particular state of mind of the composer. Such linkages are contingent, and dependent in every case on the possession of some extra-musical knowledge of the composer's life. In itself, humor in a piece of music no more guarantees the presence of bitterness than it invariably betrays a carefree state of mind. Paralleling the distinction between syntactic forms A and B, the expressive qualities of a work of art are logically independent of the psychological states of the artist, and humor (or sadness) in a madrigal is neither necessary nor sufficient for amusement (or despair) in a Monteverdi.

Thus, even where we speak of a piece of music as an expression (B) of some state of mind, this use fails to meet the requirements of the *E-T*. There is no direct, noncontingent relation between qualities of the work and states of the artist as the *E-T* supposes (F and Q are not related in the required way). The relation is contingent and mediated by extra-musical considerations, including in some instances appeal to psychological theories. Secondly, it is often *impossible* to impart a feeling quality to a work which will perceptually reflect the artist's feeling state (e.g. disappointment). And, finally, the presence of an expressive quality in a work of art is never sufficient to guarantee the presence of an analogous feeling state in the artist. What the music "expresses" is logically independent of what, if anything, the composer expresses.[32]

It follows from this that statements of the form, 'The music expresses ϕ,' or 'The music is expressive of ϕ' must, if we are to understand them as making relevant remarks about the music and not as making elliptical remarks about the composer, be interpreted as intensionally equivalent to syntactic form A; that is, they are to be understood as propositions containing 'expression' or 'expressive' as syntactic parts of a one-place predicate denoting some perceptible quality, aspect, or *gestalt* of the work itself. Moreover, 'The *music* expresses ϕ' cannot be inter-

---

[32] Many of these points may be extended beyond music, though I am not concerned to argue here for the applicability of all of these remarks to the other arts. Freud's analysis of Leonardo, for example, makes use of certain features of the paintings (the similarity of facial expression in the *Gioconda* and the *Madonna and Child with St. Anne*; the incompleteness of many of the canvases, etc.); yet none of Freud's analytic inferences are based on qualities of the paintings alone. They are rooted in his interpretation of the available biographical material. I would suggest, though I cannot pursue it here, that inferences from works of art *alone*—whether from music, fiction, or architecture—to the character of the artist are generally suspect.

THE CONCEPT OF EXPRESSION

preted as an instance of the use of 'expression' (*B*) since it would make no sense to ask for the *intentional object* of the music. The sadness of the music is not sadness *over* or *about* anything.[33] I am not claiming that everyone who uses these constructions does in fact understand them to have this meaning, but I am contending that this is the only interpretation which is both coherent and which preserves the aesthetic relevance of such assertions.

6 | To RECAPITULATE, neither playing expressively nor composing "expressive" music entails that one *be* expressing anything.[34] They require only that the product of the relevant activity have certain phenomenal properties that can be characterized as noninferentially expressive. And once we have shed the tendency to look behind the expressive qualities in an art object for some correlated act of expression we shall be closer to a correct understanding of the relation of the artist to his work; or rather, we shall be relieved at least of a persistent misunderstanding of that relation. Musicians, and artists generally, do not "express" themselves in their work in any sense that is intelligible, consistent, and aesthetically relevant. This is not to say that there is no relation between the artist's

[33] Much has been made of the difference between "real" feelings and "aesthetic" feelings; between, for instance, life-sadness and music-sadness; and I would suggest that at least the promise of an explanation lies in the fact that intentional objects are present in the former and absent from the latter.

[34] There is a trivial sense in which these activities may always be an expression of something—an expression of the desire to get the phrase right, for instance—but such expressions are irrelevant to the *E-T* for reasons given above.

activity and the resultant expressive qualities of the work, but rather to argue that it must be something other than that envisaged by the *E-T*. It would be less misleading, if a little archaic, to say simply that the relation is one of making or creating. The artist is not expressing something which is then infused into the work by alchemical transformation; he is making an expressive object. What he does to accomplish this remains, of course, as complex and mystifying as before, and I have nothing to add to the numerous attempts to explain the "creative process" except to argue that, whatever it may be, it is not identical with some act or process of expression.

One aspiration of aesthetics has always been to demonstrate that the creation of art works is a unique and exalted form of human activity. Even those like Dewey who have been determined to narrow the gap between art and ordinary experience reflect the urge to find something extraordinary in art. To conclude that the traditional concept of art-as-expression fails to realize this aim is not to abandon the conviction that there is something singular in the creative process; it is only to abandon a theory which fails to do justice to that conviction, and to reveal the need to give it more trenchant and persuasive formulation.

The theory that art is an or *the* expression of the human spirit is either trivial or false; for the sense in which art is an expression of a state of mind or character of the artist does not establish a relevant distinction between art and any other form of human activity, and the attempt to utilize the concept of expression to distinguish artistic or creative activity from more mundane affairs leads only to incoherence and absurdity. If there is a residue of truth in the *E-T*, it is that works of art often have expressive qualities. But so do natural objects, and there is nothing in this to compel us to the conclusion entailed by the *E-T*. The only way that we can interpret the notion of art-as-expression which is both coherent and aesthetically relevant is to construe statements referring to works of art and containing some cognate form of 'expression' as references to certain properties of the works themselves; and it is to a consideration of this class of properties that we shall turn in the final chapter.

CHAPTER V ART AND
EXPRESSION:
A PROPOSAL

1 | PHILOSOPHICAL concern with the expressive dimension of art has taken many directions, and it would serve no clear purpose to attempt to survey or assess them all, even if that were an attainable goal. Rather, the aim of the present chapter is limited to an extension of some of my earlier arguments and conclusions to the structuring of a proposal for comprehending and describing the expressive character of art works.

2 | IT IS TRANSPARENTLY evident that it would make no sense to assert that a work of art literally *had* e.g. the property anguish or longing or sadness—that it *was* anguished or sad (or else, as E. F. Carritt once remarked, we should have to cheer the poor thing up); and yet it is common enough to claim that an art work is *expressive of* anguish or longing or sadness. And we have seen in the preceding chapter that there are good reasons for taking 'is expressive of _____,' not as a relational predicate linking an art work to something external to it, but as an incomplete one-place predicate which, properly completed, is descriptive of some feature of the art work. It will be convenient to refer to the properties denoted by predicates of this sort as *expressive properties*. Thus, a work expressive of anguish will be said to have the *expressive* property anguish rather than simply the property anguish, the modification serving both to indicate affinities with instances where 'anguish' has unqualified application and to obviate absurdities engendered by taking art to exhibit full-blooded sentient states. The question then be-

127

comes one of establishing the connection between a property γ and the expressive property γ and explaining the apparent fact that expressive properties are not merely garden variety properties belonging to special classes of objects.

The analysis developed in earlier parts of this study suggests the following proposal: expressive properties are those properties of art works (or natural objects) whose names also designate intentional states of persons. Thus 'tenderness,' 'sadness,' 'anguish,' and 'nostalgia' may denote expressive properties of art works because they also denote states of persons that are intentional, and thus expressible in the fullest and clearest sense. This proposal imposes limitations on what shall be counted as an expressive property, and to that extent is to be regarded as a stipulation. But it is a stipulation that I believe can be defended and shown to have important advantages over alternative ways of understanding the expressive dimension of art.

Restricting our attention to art works then, an expressive property γ will be understood to be any property of an art work denoted by a predicate which also denotes intentional states of persons. Nonexpressive properties will constitute a complementary class defined merely by exclusion. (That duration, pitch, color, weight, being-the-portrait-of-X, being-a-six-voice-motet, and the like, are nonexpressive properties of art works is evident from the fact that none of these properties are designated by predicates which also denote intentional states of persons.) The dichotomy is rough-hewn and cuts across distinctions that are common in aesthetic analysis, but it will enable us to raise some important questions about the internal relations among properties commonly ascribed to art works.

3 | THE RELATION between the expressive and the nonexpressive properties of an art work is obviously an intimate one. Ravel's *Pavane pour une infante défunte* is often characterized as tender or nostalgic, and these expressive properties are dependent, in some way, upon such nonexpressive properties of the piece as the contour of the melodic line, the quasi-modal harmonic structure, the moderate tempo, and the limited dynamic range. Similarly, the animated opening bars of "Parade" from Benjamin Britten's *Les Illuminations*, though not expressive *of* animation, can be heard as expressive of apprehension, and apprehension would be an expressive property of the piece.

It is this relation between expressive and nonexpressive properties that I intend to explore, and in virtue of which I shall suggest that art works can be thought of as autonomously self-expressive objects, viz. that the complex of relations among the properties of an art work is such that it can be seen as presenting some of its properties and revealing others; those properties which are its expressive properties themselves being revealed through the presentation of varying sets of nonexpressive properties.[1]

[1] Guy Sircello, in an interesting article, "Perceptual Acts and Pictorial Art: A Defense of Expression Theory," *Journal of Philosophy*, LXII (1965), 669-77, reaches what seems to me a view similar to this, though it is stated and developed quite differently. There are limitations to Sircello's position, however, that I should

All this of course demands both clarification and defense; and we have first to justify the retention of an expression vocabulary to characterize the relation. The choice results in part from the elimination of alternatives. The relation between expressive and nonexpressive properties is more intimate than would be implied by reference to necessary conditions, critical warrants, or rule-governed regularities, all of which leave open the possibility that the relata are logically independent. But more positive reasons can be derived from arguments presented earlier for taking the behavioral and linguistic expressions of a person to be *partially constitutive* of his intentional states (Chapter II). It was argued there that certain observable aspects of behavior are logically proper parts of the complex referents of such predicates as 'anger,' 'jealousy,' 'joy,' and 'fear,' and thus partially constitutive of the intentional states denoted by predicates of this sort. And since we have already stipulated that expressive properties of art works are the aesthetic correlates of intentional

---

not like to accept. Aside from the difficulty of conceiving of expressiveness as arising from "virtual acts of perception" which occur in the art work but which are admittedly performed by no one, acts of perception—virtual or otherwise—are not among the things that can sensibly be said to be *expressed* (see Ch. 1). Also, Sircello's claims are supported entirely by reference to representational art works, and it is doubtful whether the argument, even if sound, could be extrapolated to account for the expressiveness of nonrepresentational art works. Apparently, also, on Sircello's view an art work may express such things as truthfulness and frankness, though no justification is given for regarding these as specifically *expressive* (or expressible) properties. On my view, of course, they are not expressive properties since 'truthfulness' and 'frankness' do not denote intentional states of persons.

states of persons, it follows that the relation between non-expressive and expressive properties of art works is analo-gous to the relation between human (or animal) behavior and the intentional states of which the behavior is partially constitutive.

The aesthetic situation is analogous, however, with the important difference that the nonexpressive properties of an art work are *wholly* constitutive of its expressive prop-erties, there being no "inner" aspects of art comparable to the ostensibly private states of persons. And since there is nothing "hidden" from us in an art work, there is no room for the construction of inferences from some of its properties to others. (There is nothing *essentially* private in an art work, but what is not essentially private need not be essentially obvious. Significant works of art have a per-ceptual thickness, and the critical task is to see *into* them, not through them or beyond them.) To recall an example, the tempo, dynamics, harmonic texture, melodic contour of Ravel's *Pavane* are not merely the grounds, warrants or criteria for asserting that the work is tender, they are the *constituents* of its tenderness. This relation of constitu-ency is the aesthetic analogue of the expression of full-blooded intentional states of persons, and furnishes, I be-lieve, at least provisional justification for describing art works as self-expressive objects ('*self*-expressive' to pre-vent relapse into the language of the Expression theory with the attendant implications that what is expressed be-longs to something, or someone, other than the work it-self). The tenderness of the *Pavane* and the apprehensive-ness of "Parade" are properties of the works themselves

131

expressed in, or through, the differing complexes of tempo, texture, and structure.

A serious difficulty may appear to arise here, for if a given set $[c]$ of nonexpressive properties is wholly constitutive of an expressive property γ it might appear that $[c]$ is equivalent to a set of necessary and sufficient conditions for γ. And it would follow from this that we should need only to establish the presence of $[c]$ in a particular work to conclude that it was necessarily expressive of γ, since $[c]$ would entail γ. But it has been persuasively and plausibly denied that such sets of conditions can be assumed to exist, on the grounds that it would render the detection of expressive properties a quasi-mechanical process available to anyone with normal perception, and obviate the need to develop particular aesthetic sensibilities, or to exhibit good "taste" as opposed to good sight or good hearing.[2]

However, it would be a mistake to assume that the present argument implies an equivalence of $[c]$ with a set of necessary and sufficient conditions for γ. For such an equivalence to hold, $[c]$ must be unambiguously correlated with γ. But the relation between sets of nonexpressive properties and the expressive properties of art works is such that a given set of nonexpressive properties may be compatible with, and constitutive of, any one of a *range* of expressive properties, just as a given set of gestures or movements may be compatible with (and partially constitutive of) more than one intentional state of a person. That is, $[c]$ will not be uniquely constitutive of γ; and

[2] Most effectively by Sibley in "Aesthetic Concepts."

thus, while the nonexpressive properties of an art work are wholly constitutive of its expressive properties they are *ambiguously* constitutive. And this ambiguity is the source of our inability to determine decisively whether, for example, the Ravel *Pavane* is more truly expressive of tenderness or of yearning or of nostalgia, since all of these may fall within the compatibility range of the work's nonexpressive properties. Moreover, the ambiguity is symmetrical. Not only will [c] be compatible with more than one expressive property, but more than one work may be justifiably described as tender without it following that they possess identical sets of nonexpressive properties. In consequence, the relation is not one of necessary and sufficient conditions nor of sufficient conditions alone, and no encouragement is lent to the fear (or the hope) that rule books and check lists will replace the exercise of "taste" and herald the triumph of the philistine.

Consequently, moreover, it will not do to attempt to explain the relation between expressive and nonexpressive properties as a rule-governed relation of the form: Whenever [c], predication of 'γ' is warranted. And this is not only, as is frequently argued, because no such rules can be formulated in practice, but rather because *any* rule of this sort would fail to provide for the two most relevant features of the relation. The concept of a rule-governed relation is at once too weak and too strong—too weak because it fails to account for constituency and too strong because it fails to allow for ambiguity. More generally, the language of rules, conditions, and criteria is simply inadequate to capture the relation we are considering.

4 | I HAVE ARGUED that the relation between the nonexpressive and the expressive properties of an art work is one of ambiguous constituency. There are good reasons, moreover, for believing that the resultant expressive ambiguity is essentially uneliminable and that, consequently, critical disagreements of at least one sort are, of necessity, irresoluble.

There are no uniquely decisive procedures for adjudicating between critical judgments that a work W displaying the set $[c]$ of nonexpressive properties is expressive of γ rather than δ, or δ rather than θ, so long as the relevant grounds for such claims are recognized to lie in the work itself, and as long as $[c]$ remains compatible with a range of expressive properties which includes γ, δ, and θ.[3]

Moreover we cannot confirm, or disconfirm, claims about the expressive properties of art works in the same way we frequently confirm claims that a *person* is expressing a particular intentional state. There is no access to independent evidence comparable to a person's avowals of his feelings or his subsequent behavior. Paintings, unlike people, remain silent in the face of our persistent misjudgments of them; and the possibility of disagreement

---

[3] The membership of particular compatibility ranges is flexible and subject to continuous revision, as we can note from the commonplaces of art history and art criticism. We now "see" Bambara antelope figures in ways in which no one would have seen them before Cézanne and Modigliani, and we "hear" the Mahler symphonies quite differently after exposure to Schoenberg and Stockhausen. The actual membership of particular compatibility ranges must of course be determined by aesthetic or critical judgment and not by philosophical theory.

over the expressive properties of art works remains essentially and necessarily open.

It may be suggested that there are, after all, means available to us for eliminating or accommodating critical disputes resting on the expressive ambiguity of art works. We may be tempted, for example, to resolve the issue by conceding that a work has *all* the expressive properties falling within the relevant compatibility range. But this is an excessively generous concession, and it is open to the objection that *some* of the expressive properties falling within a particular compatibility range may be psychologically or aesthetically incongruent. It might be extremely difficult to say, for instance, of a particular drawing by Käthe Kollwitz whether it was expressive of despair, anxiety, resignation, or fear. But to attempt to resolve the difficulty by attributing to the work a conjunction of such properties, or predicating of it some complex property ⟨despair-anxiety-resignation-fear⟩ would not only be to abandon all efforts at critical discrimination, it would do violence to our common understanding of these qualities. The converse alternative would be to assign members of the compatibility range of expressive properties disjunctively to the work. This, however, while logically inoffensive, is also aesthetically pointless. One must make critical choices *within* the range of available predicates, and it could hardly be thought aesthetically enlightening to be told that the Kollwitz drawing was actually expressive of ⟨despair or anxiety or resignation or fear⟩. Expressive ambiguity can neither be eliminated nor accommodated by such critical strategy, and resort to either conjunctive or disjunctive descriptions of the expressive properties of art works is an evasion and not a resolution of the critical problem.

There is a further and perhaps more decisive reason for believing the expressive ambiguity of many art works to be essentially uneliminable. The expressive "gestures" of art often occur in an aesthetic space devoid of explicit context and intentional objects. And it is the absence or the elusiveness of intentional objects that impedes our critical attempts to dissolve the ambiguity and disclose an unequivocal expressive quality in the art work. It may be true that we cannot tell from a smile, isolated from its context, whether it is a smile of parental benevolence directed toward a sleeping child or a smile of sadistic satisfaction directed toward a suffering victim.[4] But these are uncertainties that could theoretically be resolved by uncovering the intentional context. In contrast, many art works are intentionally incomplete. There are no further contexts to be uncovered and no intentional objects to be disclosed. We are free of course to invent contexts, to wrap the art work in fictions that would yield intentional objects. But is one invention more accurate, one fiction closer to the truth than another? Is there any question of *justifying* our inventions? The resolution of expressive ambiguity would require that there were.

It is not a contingent failing of art or ourselves that we frequently cannot discover what the expressive gestures

---

[4] Cf. Wittgenstein, *Philosophical Investigations*, paragraph 539, p. 145e.

of a work are *about* (toward, for, against, etc.); it is a common and aesthetically relevant condition of much of our art. Consider, for example, the expressive ambiguity of the vocabulary of modern dance movements isolated from specific dramatic contexts. Abstract dance forms consisting of context-neutral series and clusters of such movements are no less expressive than the explicitly narrative patterns of classical ballet; they are only more ambiguously expressive.[5] And there are innumerable works of art of which it would be pointless even to raise the question of intentional contexts or intentional objects —of Miro's *Painting, 1933* or the trio sonata from *The Musical Offering*, for example, and this should strengthen the suspicion that whatever expressive ambiguity such works display is not an aesthetic flaw but an inherent condition.

Now, in contrast with Baroque trio sonatas, abstract dance forms, and much contemporary visual art, many art works commonly classed as representational present us with intentional contexts (contexts in which intentional objects can be identified) as integral parts of their content. Most theatrical works exemplify this. In Euripides we are shown not only the tears of Medea; we are shown what the tears are about. In this respect Greek tragedy and Baroque instrumental music are worlds apart. The world of the drama encompasses intentional objects while the world of the trio sonata precludes them.

To the extent that intentional contexts are available

---

[5] They may also of course be merely expressive in the intransitive sense discussed in Ch. IV.

then it might appear that expressive ambiguity can be cir-
cumscribed or decisively removed. But the appearance is
chimerical. In works of representational art we can, and
should, distinguish between the expressive properties *of*
the work and contained or represented expressions *in* the
work. Among the things a representational art work may
represent are acts of expression, and failure to distinguish
between represented acts of expression and expressive
properties of the work itself will generate crucial confu-
sions. It has been said, for example, of Bernini's *David*
that it expresses a concentrated and intense determination.
But this is misleading. The *work* does not express this,
David does. The Bernini work *represents* David-express-
ing-intense-determination. And it does not follow from
this that intense determination is an expressive property
of the work itself. It does not follow that it is *not* an expressive property of the work either. Identical predicates
may apply to work and represented content alike, but each
predication is independent of the other, and false hopes
for regenerating a corollary of classical expression theories
may arise here if there is failure to notice the ellipsis when
one goes on (incorrectly) to describe the work itself as
expressing David's determination.

There is a limited though instructive parallel between
this situation and that of the actor. It was argued earlier
(Chapter II, Section 3) that it would be a distortion to
describe an actor portraying Lear as expressing Lear's
grief and despair—that we should say rather that he was
portraying or representing Lear-expressing-Lear's-despair.
And where an action is both an expression and a repre-

138

sentation of an expression we have grounds for distinguishing between actor and character as discrete logical subjects of the expressions. Now art works, like actors, may portray *inter alia* acts of expression; and in both cases distortions will be avoided only if reference to represented expressions is distinguished from reference to properties correctly attributable only to the representing *agency*—the actor or the art work.

In general, it is only the contained or represented expression whose ambiguity is dissolved by the availability of intentional contexts in the art work. We may, given the circumstances of the action of a drama, be justifiably certain that the cries of the protagonist are an expression of remorse, but this leaves unanswered the question of the expressive properties of the *play*. The drama itself may project pity, horror, or contempt toward the remorse of the protagonist. That is, it may have as one of *its* expressive properties pity, horror, or contempt, and thereby comment expressively on the represented acts of expression. Acts of expression cannot themselves be expressed in art, but they can be depicted, described, reflected upon, or judged, and all these possibilities lie within the province of one or several of the representational arts. The distinction we have been considering should in fact explain the capacity of representational arts, generally, to make expressive comments on their represented content. While the availability of intentional contexts may help to obviate ambiguity in the represented expressions then, it may do little or nothing to alleviate critical discord resting on the expressive ambiguity of an art work itself, even where the work is incontestably representational and contains intentional contexts as an integral part of its content.

5 | EXPRESSIVE ambiguity is an inherent feature of most if not all of our art. And it is a continuing dilemma of critical practice that we are faced with the necessity of making and defending choices from a range of available alternatives for describing the expressive character of particular art works—choices that must be made in the absence of any clearly decisive means for eliminating alternative and competing descriptions. This dilemma is, I believe, inescapable since it rests on the aesthetic need for making *some* critical choices conjoined with the impossibility of establishing the necessity for making just those choices that we do make. And it is this that makes the exercise of critical judgment so intriguing to those whose tolerance for indeterminacy is high and so frustrating to those for whom the quest for certainty is always paramount.

FINALLY, then, to the extent that our aesthetic concerns are with the expressive dimension of art, I would suggest that art works be thought of as ambiguously self-expressive objects. The virtue I would like to claim for this way of thinking of art is that it commits us to neither of the disjuncts of the prevalent assumption that a reference to expression in art is either (*a*) a reference to something lying behind or beyond the work—a thought, feeling, mood, or attitude to which the work stands in some external relation—or (*b*) a reference to something immedi-

140

ately presented to perception as an aesthetic "surface." There are, I think, decisive objections to this antithesis. If the argument of Chapter IV is correct, critical appreciation of the expressiveness of an art work is clearly not an inductive or an inferential procedure. It does not follow, however, that if we are not engaged in searching out something behind the art work then its expressiveness must lie openly and obviously on the surface; for if that were the case, we would be at a loss to explain the continuing divergence of informed judgment concerning the expressive qualities of art works.

The alternatives have been misstated. Discerning the expressive properties of art is neither a matter of scanning surfaces with the naïve eye nor sounding hidden depths with delicate inference tools, and the conception of art works as ambiguously self-expressive objects offers at least an escape from the correlative mistakes of the antithesis and, hopefully, a more promising way of both elucidating the expressive dimension of art and of accounting for the legitimacy of critical disagreement. The discerning of expressive properties requires the fusion of perception and choice. And that is perhaps, after all, what is entailed in the exercise of taste.

APPENDIX

THE FOLLOWING extracts are representative samples from the writings of some of the more prominent Expression theorists. Despite differences in detail and emphasis they all exemplify the *E-T* formulated in Chapter IV. Dewey has been omitted since there are extensive quotations from *Art as Experience* in the text.

1 | FROM *The Principles of Art* by R. G. Collingwood (Oxford: Clarendon Press, 1938). Reprinted by permission of the publisher.

Our first question is this. Since the artist proper has something to do with emotion, and what he does with it is not to arouse it, what is it that he does? It will be remembered that the kind of answer we expect to this question is an answer derived from what we all know and all habitually say; nothing original or recondite, but something entirely commonplace.

Nothing could be more entirely commonplace than to say he expresses them. The idea is familiar to every artist, and to every one else who has any acquaintance with the arts. To state it is not to state a philosophical theory or definition of art; it is to state a fact or supposed fact about which, when we have sufficiently identified it, we shall have later to theorize philosophically.

. . . .

Finally, the expressing of emotion must not be confused with what may be called the betraying of it, that is, exhibiting symptoms of it. When it is said that the artist in the proper sense of that word is a person who expresses his emotions, this does not mean that if he is afraid he turns pale and stammers; if he is angry he turns red and bellows; and so forth.

These things are no doubt called expressions; but just as we distinguish proper and improper senses of the word 'art', so we must distinguish proper and improper senses of the word 'expression', and in the context of a discussion about art this sense of expression is an improper sense. The characteristic mark of expression proper is lucidity or intelligibility; a person who expresses something thereby becomes conscious of what it is that he is expressing, and enables others to become conscious of it in himself and in them. Turning pale and stammering is a natural accompaniment of fear, but a person who in addition to being afraid also turns pale and stammers does not thereby become conscious of the precise quality of his emotion. About that he is as much in the dark as he would be if (were that possible) he could feel fear without also exhibiting these symptoms of it.

. . . .

If art is not a kind of craft, but the expression of emotion, this distinction . . . between artist and audience disappears. For the artist has an audience only in so far as people hear him expressing himself, and understand what they hear him saying. Now, if one person says something by way of expressing what is in his mind, and another hears and understands him, the hearer who understands him has that same thing in his mind. . . . What is here said of expressing thoughts is equally true of expressing emotions. If a poet expresses, for example, a certain kind of fear, the only hearers who can understand him are those who are capable of experiencing that kind of fear themselves. Hence, when some one reads and understands a poem, he is not merely understanding the poet's expression of his, the poet's emotions, he is expressing emotions of his own in the poet's words, which have thus become his own words. As Coleridge put it, we know a man for a poet by the fact that he makes us poets. We know that he is expressing his emotions by the fact that he is enabling us to express ours.

... The poet is not singular either in his having that emotion or in his power of expressing it; he is singular in his ability to take the initiative in expressing what all feel, and all can express.

2 | From *Art, the Critics, and You* by Curt J. Ducasse (New York: Bobbs-Merrill, 1955). Reprinted by permission of the Liberal Arts Press Division.

What Art Is Essentially

Other unsuccessful attempts to say what differentiates art from the other forms of purposive activity might be reviewed here, but the discussion of those already considered has perhaps been enough to sharpen the meaning of the problem and to provide us with a certain perspective upon it. I therefore now turn to what I conceive to be the true answer to our question. *It is that art is essentially a form of language— namely, the language of feeling, mood, sentiment, and emotional attitude.* It is thus to be distinguished from the language of assertion, which is what we use to formulate opinions, information, hypotheses, and so on. That is, what occurs in art creation is that the artist finds himself emotionally stirred—whether by something he perceives at the time or by something he thinks of, or perhaps as an effect of certain obscure psychological or physiological causes—and attempts to express the feeling that inspires him by creating an object that "embodies" it.

The Objectification of Feeling

Objective expression, in the case of the language of feeling, means substantially the same thing as in the language of assertion. When we do what is called "putting our thought into words," we do not put it in in the literal sense in which we put water into a bucket. What we do is to create an object —specifically, a sentence—in which the thought is "embodied" or "objectified," in the sense that from it, by reading, the thought that dictated the words can be recovered. Similarly, in the case of art, objective expression of a feeling means that an object is created—an arrangement of color shapes perhaps, or of tones, and so on—from which, through contemplation, can be obtained back the feeling of which that object is itself the expression. The faithfulness with which the object reflects that feeling is the measure of the adequacy with which it has been objectified.

. . . .

The feeling that initially inspires the artist to begin a particular work is best thought of as a seed, so to speak, of the total feeling ultimately expressed. The latter is present in the former only in the sense of being the final unfoldment of the specific potentialities—the natural proliferation—of that particular initial feeling.

What, in the great majority of cases, actually takes place is that the initial feeling moves the artist to some relatively simple creative acts; that he then contemplates the result of these acts; that out of this there arises a growth of his feeling that inspires him to certain additional creative strokes; that he then again contemplates what he has so far done; and so on, over and over again until the work attains its final form.

3 | From *The Philosophy of Art* by Curt J. Ducasse (New York: Dover, 1966). Reprinted by permission of the publisher.

Aesthetic art, which is what usually is referred to when the word Art is used without qualification, is the conscious objectification of one's feelings.

. . . .

What is meant here by speaking of objectification, or of expression as objective, is that the act of expression is (in such a case) creative of something (1) capable of being contemplated by the artist at least, and (2) such that *in contemplation that thing yields back to him the feeling, meaning, or volition of which it was the attempted expression.*

.   .   .   .

I do not by any means contend that the emotion which the artist expresses through art-creation cannot be an effect or resultant, more or less direct, of some situation that he faces. On the contrary, that is often the fact. But it is a fact which in no way alters the nature of art as objectification of emotion. How the artist came by the emotion which he objectifies is an interesting question perhaps, but it is one wholly irrelevant to that of the nature of art. As concerns that, the only important facts are that the artist has first an emotion to express, and then does employ material through which to express it; and that he expresses it not in the utilitarian way, (which deals with the object of the emotion), but by creating something which objectifies, i.e., mirrors back, the emotion.

.   .   .   .

. . . art is not merely self-expression, nor even merely objective self-expression, but *consciously* objective self-expression. . . . One must be able to acknowledge the product as an adequate statement of oneself.

.   .   .   .

It may be pointed out in the first place that the definition given distinguishes expressions of feeling which are art from those which, like yawning, laughing, stretching, etc., are not art. The character which truly distinguishes art from such other expressions of feeling is the critical control in respect to objectivity, which is an intrinsic part of art; . . .

4 | From *Art and the Social Order* by D. W. Gotshalk (New York: Dover, 1962). Reprinted by permission of the publisher.

While universal abstract expressiveness may occur in a work possessing only a presentational level, representation can occur, of course, only in a work of art possessing a representational, as well as a presentational, level. The two other major types of artistic expressiveness deserving special mention, however, can occur both in representational and in merely presentational artistic creations.

The first is the expression of the personality of the artist or, more precisely, of his character as a technician and as a man. In nonrepresentational works this can be suggested by the sort of materials that the artist selects and emphasizes, by the way his presentational designs are built, by the abstract expressive content that he reiterates or underlines, and by the aims or goals or functions of his works. In representational art, it can be suggested by the interpretation of the subject embodied in the representation, as well as by the factors just mentioned. From all these clues an imaginative percipient can often obtain very vivid suggestions of the characteristic manner or technique of the artist and the individual scale of values and telic inclinations of the man. Literally, of course, neither technique nor scale of values and telic inclinations are in the public object. The technique is a feature of the antecedent creative process, the cause from which the public object springs as effect. The scale of values and the telic inclinations are literally possessions of the artist, who controlled the creative process of which the public object is the effect. Nevertheless, suggestions of, or clues to, these causo-telic factors become deeply imprinted upon the public object just because the artist by his technique, inclinations, and scale of values has shaped this object as his effect. And, with imagination, a percipient can apprehend these clues as properties of the public object suggestive of the artist as technician and as man.

. . . .

148

... the world of art is one in which the artist usually can command, far more successfully than in almost any other region of his experience, the type of effect that satisfies his nature. In this world he is ordinarily more at home, and more free, as well as more able, to achieve a realization of deeply cherished aspirations. That his creations should therefore record and suggest to a considerable extent the slant of his being and the value inclinations of his nature seems logical and inevitable, since usually these are given fullest expression where one can attain in a superior degree a fulfilment of one's deeply cherished aspirations.

5 | From *What is Art? and Essays on Art*, by Leo Tolstoy, tr. Aylmer Maude (New York: Oxford, 1962). Reprinted by permission of the publisher.

Every work of art causes the receiver to enter into a certain kind of relationship both with him who produced or is producing the art, and with all those who, simultaneously, previously, or subsequently, receive the same artistic impression.

Speech transmitting the thoughts and experiences of men serves as a means of union among them, and art serves a similar purpose. The peculiarity of this latter means of intercourse, distinguishing it from intercourse by means of words, consists in this, that whereas by words a man transmits his thoughts to another, by art he transmits his feelings.

The activity of art is based on the fact that a man receiving through his sense of hearing or sight another man's expression of feeling, is capable of experiencing the emotion which moved the man who expressed it. To take the simplest example: one man laughs, and another who hears becomes merry, or a man weeps, and another who hears feel sorrow. A man is excited or irritated, and another man seeing him is brought to a similar state of mind. By his movements or by the sounds of his voice a man expresses courage and determination or sadness and calmness, and this state of mind passes on to others. A man suffers, manifesting his sufferings by groans and spasms, and this suffering transmits itself to other people; a man expresses his feelings of admiration, devotion, fear, respect, or love, to certain objects, persons, or phenomena, and others are infected by the same feelings of admiration, devotion, fear, respect, or love, to the same objects, persons, or phenomena.

And it is on this capacity of man to receive another man's expression of feeling and to experience those feelings himself, that the activity of art is based.

. . . .

To evoke in oneself a feeling one has once experienced and having evoked it in oneself then by means of movements, lines, colours, sounds, or forms expressed in words, so to transmit that feeling that others experience the same feeling —this is the activity of art.

Art is a human activity consisting in this, that one man consciously by means of certain external signs, hands on to others feelings he has lived through, and that others are infected by these feelings and also experience them.

. . . .

I have mentioned three conditions of contagion in art, but they may all be summed up into one, the last, sincerity; that is, that the artist should be impelled by an inner need to express his feeling. That condition includes the first; for if the artist is sincere he will express the feeling as he experienced it. And as each man is different from every one else, his feeling will be individual for every one else; and the more individual it is—the more the artist has drawn it from the depths of his nature—the more sympathetic and sincere will it be.

150

And this same sincerity will impel the artist to find clear expression for the feeling which he wishes to transmit.

6 | FROM *Aesthetics* by Eugene Véron, tr. W. H. Armstrong (London: 1879).

We may say then, by way of general definition, that art is the manifestation of emotion, obtaining external interpretation, now by expressive arrangements of line, form or color, now by a series of gestures, sounds, or words governed by particular rhythmical cadence.

. . . .

What We Admire in a Work of Art is the Genius of the Artist.

The more of this personal character that a work possesses; the more harmonious its details and their combined expression; the more clearly each part communicates the impression of the artist, whether of grandeur, of melancholy or of joy; in fine, the more that expression of human sensation and will predominates over mere imitation, the better will be its chance of obtaining sooner or later the admiration of the world—always supposing that the sentiment expressed be a generous one, and that the execution be not of such a kind as to repel or baffle connoisseurs.

. . . .

The chief characteristic of modern art—of art, that is, left to follow its own inspiration free from academic patronage—is power of expression. . . .

Art, thus understood, demands from its votary an ensemble of intellectual faculties higher and more robust than if founded solely upon an ideal of beauty. Art founded upon the latter notion would be sufficiently served by one possessing an acute sense of the beautiful—the degree of his sensibility being indicated by the plastic perfection of his work. But expressive art demands a capability of being moved by many varying sentiments, demands the power to penetrate beneath outward appearances and to seize a hidden thought, the power to grasp either the permanent characteristic or the particular and momentary emotion; in a word, it demands that complete eloquence of representation which art might have dispensed with while it confined itself to the investigation of delineation of a single expression, but which became absolutely indispensable from the moment that the interpretation of the entire man became its avowed object.

. . . .

The necessity for this is one consequence of the distinction which we have established between decorative and expressive art. The former, solely devoted to the gratification of eye and ear, affords no measure of its success beyond the pleasure which it gives. The latter, whose chief object is to express the feelings and ideas, and, through them, to manifest the power of conception and expansion possessed by the artist, must obviously be estimated, partly at least, by the moral or other value of the ideas and sentiments in question. And, as the value of a work depends directly upon the capability of its author, and as many artists have been about equal in their technical ability, we must be ready to acknowledge that moral and intellectual superiority is a real superiority, and is naturally marked by the possession of an instinctive and spontaneous power of sympathy.

. . . .

We think ourselves justified, then, in calling art the direct and spontaneous manifestation of human personality. But we must not omit also to remember the fact that personality—individual and particular as it is from some points of view—is nevertheless exposed to many successive and temporary modifications caused by the various kinds of civilization through which it has had to pass.

SELECTED BIBLIOGRAPHY

Allport, G. W., and Vernon, P. E. *Studies in Expressive Movement*. New York: Macmillan, 1933.

Alston, William. "Expressing." *Philosophy in America*. Ed. Max Black. Ithaca: Cornell, 1965.

Anscombe, G.E.M. "Pretending." *Proceedings of the Aristotelian Society, Supplementary Volume* XXXII (1958), 279-94.

Arnheim, Rudolf. *Art and Visual Perception: A Psychology of the Creative Eye*. Berkeley and Los Angeles: University of California Press, 1954.

———. "The Gestalt Theory of Expression." *Psychological Review*, LVI (1949), 156-71.

Asch, Solomon. *Social Psychology*. Englewood Cliffs: Prentice-Hall, 1952.

Austin, J. L. *How to Do Things with Words*. Ed. J. O. Urmson. A Galaxy Book, New York: Oxford, 1965.

———. "Other Minds." *Philosophical Papers*. Eds. J. O. Urmson and G. J. Warnock. Oxford: Clarendon, 1961.

Beardsley, Monroe C. *Aesthetics: Problems in the Philosophy of Criticism*. New York: Harcourt Brace & World, 1958.

Bedford, Errol. "Emotions." *Proceedings of the Aristotelian Society*, LVII (1956-57), 281-304.

Benson, John. "Emotion and Expression." *Philosophical Review*, LXXVI (1967), 335-58.

Bloomfield, L. *Language*. New York: Holt, 1946.

Bouwsma, O. K. "The Expression Theory of Art." *Philosophical Analysis*. Ed. Max Black. Ithaca: Cornell, 1950.

Britton, Karl. "Feelings and Their Expression." *Philosophy*, xxxii (1957), 97-111.

Broadbent, D. E. *Behavior*. London: Eyre and Spottiswoode, 1961.

Campbell-Fisher, Ivy. "Intrinsic Expressiveness." *Journal of General Psychology*, xlv (1951), 3-24.

Candland, Douglas K., ed. *Emotion: Bodily Change*. New York: Van Nostrand, 1962.

Carnap, Rudolf. *Philosophy and Logical Syntax*. London: Kegan Paul, Trench, Trubner, 1935.

Carritt, E. F. *What Is Beauty?* Oxford: Clarendon, 1932.

Chisholm, Roderick. "Intentionality and the Theory of Signs." *Philosophical Studies*, iii (1952), 56-63.

———. *Perceiving*. Ithaca: Cornell, 1957.

———. ed. *Realism and the Background of Phenomenology*. New York: The Free Press, 1960.

Collingwood, R. C. *The Principles of Art*. Oxford: Clarendon, 1938.

Croce, Benedetto. *Aesthetic as Science of Expression and General Linguistic*. Tr. Douglas Ainslie. 2d ed. London: Macmillan, 1922.

Danto, Arthur. "The Artworld." *Journal of Philosophy*, lxi (1964), 571-84.

Darwin, Charles. *The Expression of the Emotions in Man and Animals*. Phoenix Books, Chicago: University of Chicago Press, 1965.

Dewey, John. *Art as Experience*. New York: Putnam's, 1934.

Donagan, Alan. "Wittgenstein on Sensation." *Wittgenstein: The Philosophical Investigations*. Ed. George Pitcher. Anchor Books, New York: Doubleday, 1966.

Ducasse, Curt John. *The Philosophy of Art*. New York: Dover, 1966.

Garvin, Lucius. "Emotivism, Expression and Symbolic Meaning." *Journal of Philosophy*, LV (1958), 112-18.

Geach, P. T. "Assertion." *Philosophical Review*, LXXIV (1965), 449-65.

―――. *Mental Acts: Their Content and Their Objects*. London: Routledge & Kegan Paul; New York: Humanities Press, 1957.

Gombrich, E. H. *Art and Illusion: A Study in the Psychology of Pictorial Representation*. (The A. W. Mellon Lectures in the Fine Arts, 1956.) Bollingen Series XXXV, 5. New York: Pantheon, 1960.

―――. *Meditations on a Hobby Horse: and Other Essays on the Theory of Art*. London: Phaidon, 1963.

Goodman, Nelson. *Languages of Art: An Approach to a Theory of Symbols*. New York: Bobbs-Merrill, 1968.

Gosling, J. C. "Emotion and Object." *Philosophical Review*, LXXIV (1965), 486-503.

Gregor, A. James. "Psychoanalytic Disposition Terms and Reduction Sentences." *Journal of Philosophy*, LXIII (1966), 737-45.

Gurney, Edmund. *The Power of Sound*. London: Smith, Elder, 1880.

Hampshire, Stuart. *Feeling and Expression*. London: H. K. Lewis, 1961.

———. *Thought and Action*. New York: Viking, 1960.

Hanslick, Eduard. *The Beautiful in Music*. Tr. Gustav Cohen. Ed. Morris Weitz. A Liberal Arts Press Book, New York: Bobbs-Merrill, 1957.

Hartshorne, Charles. *The Philosophy and Psychology of Sensation*. Chicago: University of Chicago Press, 1934.

Hebb, D. O. *The Organization of Behavior*. New York: Wiley, 1949.

Hindemith, Paul. *A Composer's World*. Cambridge: Harvard, 1952.

Hofstadter, Albert. *Truth and Art*. New York: Columbia, 1965.

Hospers, John. "The Concept of Artistic Expression." *Proceedings of the Aristotelian Society*, LV (1954-55), 313-44.

Hungerland, Isabel. "Iconic Signs and Expressiveness." *Journal of Aesthetics and Art Criticism*, III (n.d.), 15-21.

Kenny, Anthony. *Action, Emotion and Will*. London: Routledge & Kegan Paul; New York: Humanities Press, 1963.

———. "Cartesian Privacy." *Wittgenstein: The Philosophical Investigations*. Ed. George Pitcher. Anchor Books, New York: Doubleday, 1966.

Kivy, Peter. "Aesthetic Aspects and Aesthetic Qualities." *Journal of Philosophy*, LXV (1968), 85-93.

Kris, Ernst. *Psychoanalytic Explorations in Art*. London: Allen & Unwin, 1953.

Langer, Susanne K. *Philosophy in a New Key*. Cambridge: Harvard, 1942.

Maslow, A. H. "The Expressive Component of Behavior." *Psychological Review*, LVI (1949), 261-72.

Meyer, Leonard B. *Emotion and Meaning in Music*. Phoenix Books, Chicago: University of Chicago Press, 1961.

Plutchick, Robert. *The Emotions*. New York: Random House, 1962.

Putnam, Hilary. "Psychological Concepts, Explication, and Ordinary Language." *Journal of Philosophy*, LIV (1957), 94-100.

Quine, W.V.O. *Word and Object*. New York: Technology Press of MIT and Wiley, 1960.

Reid, L. A. "Feeling and Expression in the Arts: Expression, Sensa, and Feelings." *Journal of Aesthetics and Art Criticism*, XXV (1966), 123-35.

Santayana, George. *The Sense of Beauty*. New York: Scribner's, 1896.

Scheffler, Israel. *The Anatomy of Inquiry*. New York: Knopf, 1963.

Sibley, Frank. "Aesthetic Concepts." *Philosophical Review*, LXVIII (1959), 421-50.

Sircello, Guy. "Perceptual Acts and Pictorial Art: A Defense of Expression Theory." *Journal of Philosophy*, LXII (1965), 669-77.

Strawson, P. F. *Individuals*. Ch. III, "Persons." New York: Doubleday, 1963.

Szasz, Thomas. *Pain and Pleasure*. New York: Basic Books, 1957.

Taylor, Charles. *The Explanation of Behavior*. London: Routledge & Kegan Paul, 1964.

Tolstoy, Leo. "What is Art?" (1898). *What is Art? and Essays on Art*. Tr. Aylmer Maude. A Hespirides Book, New York: Oxford, 1962.

Tomas, Vincent A. "The Concept of Expression in Art." *Philosophy Looks at the Arts*. Ed. Joseph Margolis. New York: Scribner's, 1962.

Urmson, J. O. "Parenthetical Verbs." *Mind*, LXI (1952), 480-96.

Werner, H., ed. *On Expressive Language*. Worcester, Mass.: Clark University Press, 1955.

Wittgenstein, L. *Lectures & Conversations on Aesthetics, Psychology and Religious Belief*. Ed. Cyril Barrett. Berkeley and Los Angeles: University of California Press, 1966.

———. *Philosophical Investigations*. Tr. G.E.M. Anscombe. New York: Macmillan, 1953.

Wolff, H. G., and Hardy, J. D. "On the Nature of Pain." *Physiological Review*, XXVII (1947).

——— and Wolf, Stewart. *Pain*. Rev. ed. Springfield, Illinois: Charles C. Thomas, 1949.

Wolff, W. *The Expression of Personality*. New York: Harper, 1943.

Wollheim, Richard. *Art and Its Objects: An Introduction to Aesthetics*. New York: Harper & Row, 1968.

———. "Expression." *The Human Agent*, Royal Institute of Philosophy Lectures, Vol. i. New York: St. Martin's, 1968, 227-44.

———. "On Expression and Expressionism." *Revue Internationale De Philosophie*, LXVIII-LXIX (1964), 270-89.

Ziff, Paul. *Semantic Analysis*. Ithaca: Cornell, 1960.

INDEX

acting, 52-55, 59; and espressing, 52-55- 59, 138-39; method, 52, 55
actions, 17ff
actors, and art works, 138-39
"aesthetic expression," 102
"aesthetic" feelings, 122n33
aesthetic objects, 103, 116
aesthetic predicates, 115-16
aesthetic qualities, 102, 115, 116
aesthetic "surface," 141
Aldrich, Virgil C., 116n28
Anscombe, G.E.M., 57n
anxiety, 33-34
apologizing, 88-89, 93
art, and expression, Chaps. IV and V *passim*; and psychoanalysis, 117-18; process and product, 97-98. *See also* Expression theory of art
art objects, as autonomously self-expressive, 129
aspect-blindness, *see* aspect perception
aspect perception, 114-16
assertion, and expression, 68, 69, 70, 75
attitudes, 9, 10
Austin, J. L., 31n, 47n7, 57n, 70, 84, 85, 90, 91, 92n

Bedford, Errol, 48n
behavior, 4, 5, 43, and *passim*; ceremonial, 59n
belief, 5, 9, 10; as disposition, 69-71; as intentional state, 10-13; linguistic expression of, 68-76; as performative

utterance, 70-71; prepositional analysis of, 12-13; as psychological state, 70-71
Bennett, Jonathan, 77n16
Bernini, *David*, 138
Black, Max, 83n
Bosanquet, Bernard, 98n3
Bradley, F. H., 76
Brentano, Franz, 10n, 19n
Britten, Benjamin, *Les Illuminations*, 129, 131-32

Carnap, Rudolph, 43, 63-65, 68
Carritt, E. F., 103
Chisholm, R., 10n, 11n
Collingwood, R. G., 98, 99, 103, 143-45
conventions, 41
criticism, dilemma of, 140-41

dance forms, abstract, 137
Danto, Arthur C., 116n27
Debussy, Claude, *Prélude à 'L'Après-Midi D' Un Faune,'* 110n
depression, 33-35
description, and expression, 62-67; non-neutrality of, 45-46
Dewey, John, 97-98, 99, 100, 101, 102, 103, 123
dispositions, 9. *See also* belief
Ducasse, C. J., 33, 97-98, 99, 101n13, 103, 145-47

Edwards, Paul, 68n5
emotion, 4, 9, 10, and *passim*

161

E-operators, 80-83; and tense transformations, 81-83
epistemological neutrality, 13
espressivo, 110-13
Euripides, *Medea*, 137
exclamations, 65-67; truth-value of, 65-66
'express,' as parenthetical, 81n20
expression: antinomy of, 50-51; and causes, 8; and communication, 92-93; contingent and noncontingent, 30ff; and the creative process, 123f; descriptive/inference warranting, 40ff; facial, 55; as "forcing out," 27-28; logical asymmetry of, 39-42; misplaced, 19; projection of, 41; and representation, 53-55; secondary, 117, 120; and sincerity, 81, 88, 89, 91, 93; substitute, 76n14; as a two-term relation, 29; voluntary/involuntary, 20ff, 43-44, 101
expression-deafness, *see* aspect perception
Expression theory of art, Chap. IV *passim*; Appendix
'expressive': dispositional sense of, 108; as distinct from 'expression,' 106-110; as evaluative predicate, 112, 113; intransitive sense of, 108, 111, 112
expressive behavior, aboutness of, 22; surface of, 52ff
expressive properties, 106; Chap. V *passim*; ambiguity of, 132-41; compatibility ranges of, 132-35; conjunctive

and disjunctive sets of, 135-36; constituency of, 130-34; criterial warrants for, 130; critical disagreement over, 134-41; necessary and sufficient conditions for, 132-33; in representational art, 137-39; rule-governed regularities of, 130, 133. *See also* expressive qualities
expressive qualities, 103, 104, 118, 120, 123, 124. *See also* expressive properties

fear, "objectless," 33-35
Freud, Sigmund, 34, 118n, 121n

Gotshalk, D. W., 103, 147-49

Hampshire, Stuart, 74-75
Hardy, J. D., 25-26
Hare, R. M., 84, 86
Hebb, D. O., 8n, 23, 24, 25
hope, and intention, 78-79; expression of, 77-79
Hospers, John, 99
Husserl, E., 10n

imitation, 53
imperatives, incompatible, 110n
inference: Cartesian model, 51; causal, 45; conceptual, 47ff; and conceptual matrices, 51; and evidence, 47; and expression, 105, 109; and intentionality, 117, 118, 120; warranting of, 44ff
inferential relations, 43, 44, 45
intentional ascription, 11, 13

intentional contexts in art, 136-39
intentional implications, 46-47
intentional objects, 10, 19 and n, 20, 28n22; Chap. I *passim*; in art works, 136-39; definition of, 10-11. *See also* prepositional objects
intentional states, 42, 43, 45, 128, 129n, 130, 131, 132, 134; aesthetic correlates of, 130-31; behavior as constitutive part of, 48-51; causes and objects of, 16-17; definition of, 13. *See also* intentional objects

jealousy, 47, 48, 49
Jung, C. G., 118n

keening, 59n
Kenny, Anthony, 19n, 34, 35, 47n6
Kivy, Peter, 116n28
Kollwitz, Käthe, 135

language, Chap. III *passim*; expressive/descriptive function of, 63-67; parenthetical use of, 79-83; performative use of, 83-93
linguistic expression: and intentional states, 87; and performative utterance, 83ff

Mahler, Gustav, *Das Lied von der Erde*, 104
Morgan, C. T., 23
Music, expression in, 109-16, 118-22; expressive performance of, 109-16

Nielsen, Carl, "Sinfonia Semplice" (Symphony No. 6), 118-20
nonexpressive properties, 128-32; Chap. V *passim*

objects: immediate, virtual, and latent, 18ff; of perception, 16. *See also* intentional objects
opinion: belief and, 71-77; intentionality of, 73n9
oratio obliqua, 82-83
Osborne, Harold, 103n

pain, 23-27
perception, 4, 5, 16
physiognomic qualities, 103, 106. *See also* expressive properties
prepositional objects, 10, 11, 12. *See also* intentional objects
prepositions, transitivity and intransitivity of, 14
pretending, 56-59
promising, 71n, 85-89, 92, 93
psychological predicates, 47ff
psychological theory, 8

Quine, W.V.O., 10n

Ravel, Maurice, *Pavane pour une infante défunte*, 129, 131-32, 133
Reid, L. A., 97-98
Russell, Bertrand, 80n17

Santayana, George, 97-98, 103
Scheffler, Israel, 10n
"seeing-as," 116. *See also* aspect perception

sensations, 4, 5, 6, 7; Chap. 1
    passim
sentence surrogates, 66 and n
Sibley, Frank, 114n, 132n
signs, 29-32
Sircello, Guy, 129n
Strang, Barbara, 15n
Strawson, P. F., 47n6, 47n7
symptoms, 29
synecdoche, 48, 50
syntax, prepositional, 12f

taste, 132-33, 141

Tilghman, B. R., 116n28
Titchener, E. B., 24n
Tolstoy, Leo, 103, 149-51
Tomas, Vincent, 98-99

Urmson, J. O., 80-81

Véron, Eugene, 103, 151-52

Wittgenstein, L., 16n, 65, 77,
    116n28, 136n
Wolff, H. G., 25-26